**The Princeton Review**

D0514862

# Cracking the

# SAT®

## French
## Subject Test

## 15th Edition

Monique Gaden and Simone Ingram
and the Staff of The Princeton Review

PrincetonReview.com

**PENGUIN RANDOM HOUSE**

The Princeton Review
24 Prime Parkway, Suite 201
Natick, MA 01760
E-mail: editorialsupport@review.com

Published in the United States by Random House LLC, New York, and simultaneously in Canada by Random House of Canada Limited, Toronto.

A Penguin Random House Company.

ISBN 978-0-8041-2570-3
eBook ISBN: 978-0-8041-2571-0
ISSN: 1075-6051

Editor: Selena Coppock
Production Editors: Wendy Carroll and Lee Elder
Production Artist: Deborah A. Silvestrini

Printed in the United States of America on partially recycled paper.

10  9  8  7  6  5  4  3  2  1

15th Edition

**Editorial**

Rob Franek, Senior VP, Publisher
Casey Cornelius, VP Content Development
Mary Beth Garrick, Director of Production
Selena Coppock, Managing Editor
Calvin Cato, Editor
Colleen Day, Editor
Aaron Riccio, Editor
Meave Shelton, Editor
Orion McBean, Editorial Assistant

**Random House Publishing Team**

Tom Russell, Publisher
Alison Stoltzfus, Publishing Manager
Melinda Ackell, Associate Managing Editor
Ellen Reed, Production Manager
Kristin Lindner, Production Supervisor
Andrea Lau, Designer

# Acknowledgments

Thank you to Benjamin Young, Faculty Fellow at Columbia University, for his additional input on changes in the Vocabulary and Grammar sections of this book.

Special thanks to Adam Robinson, who conceived of and perfected the Joe Bloggs approach to standardized tests and many of the other successful techniques used by The Princeton Review.

Thank you to Adrian Sanchez for his thorough content review of this text for the 15th Edition.

# Contents

# ...So Much More Online!

## More Practice

- Free SAT online demonstration with a full-length practice SAT
- Free ACT online demonstration with a full-length practice ACT

## More Good Stuff...

- Articles about test-taking techniques to get you ready for the next step
- Opinions and advice regarding the SAT vs. ACT: which one is right for you?
- Important information about study abroad programs

## ...then College!

- Detailed profiles for hundreds of colleges help you find the school that is right for you
- Top 10 ranking lists including Quality of Professors, Worst Campus Food, Most Beautiful Campus, Party Schools, Diverse Student Population, and dozens more
- Useful information about the admissions process
- Helpful guidance about financial aid and scholarships

## Offline Resources

If you are looking for more college advice or more opportunities to review, please feel free to pick up these books in stores right now!

- *Cracking the SAT Premium, 2015 Edition*
- *Are You Ready for the SAT & ACT?*
- *Best 379 Colleges, 2015 Edition*
- *Paying For College Without Going Broke, 2015 Edition*
- *If The U Fits*

Head over to PrincetonReview.com right now!
Follow us on Twitter: @ThePrincetonRev
Questions about test changes? We've got answers! Head over to
PrincetonReview.com/SATChanges

PrincetonReview.com

### Look For These Icons Throughout The Book

Proven Techniques

More Great Books

Applied Strategies

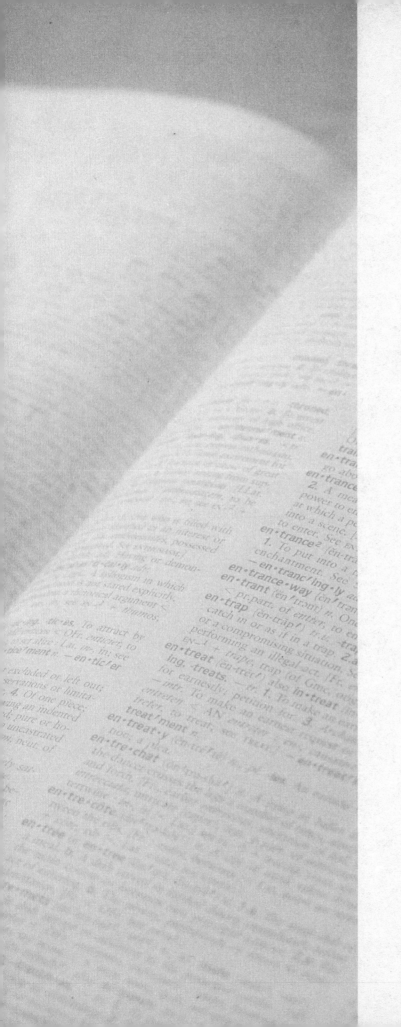

# Part I
# Orientation

# Chapter 1
# Introduction

You have chosen to take the SAT French Subject Test, and now it is time to demonstrate all you have learned during the course of your advanced study. This book will help you understand the format of the SAT French Test and will give you all the tools you need to do your best.

This book is divided into four parts. Part One gives you an orientation of the French Subject Test and reveals some basic strategies. Part Two gives you the format for each section of the test and reviews key grammar and vocabulary words. Part Three contains answers and explanations for the drills found in Part Two. Part Four contains two practice SAT French Subject Tests along with answers and explanations for each test.

# WHAT ARE THE SAT SUBJECT TESTS?

They are a series of one-hour exams developed and administered by the Educational Testing Service (ETS) and the College Board. The SAT Subject Tests are designed to measure specific knowledge in specific areas. There are many different tests in many different subject areas, such as biology, history, French, and math. They are scored separately on a 200–800 scale.

## How Are SAT Subject Tests Used by College Admissions?

Because the tests are given in specific areas, colleges use them as another piece of admissions information and, often, to decide whether an applicant can be exempted from college requirements. A good SAT French score might place you in second-year French instead of first-year French, or exempt you from a foreign language requirement altogether.

## Should I Take the SAT Subject Tests? How Many? When?

About one-third of the colleges that require SAT scores also require that you take two or three Subject Tests. Your first order of business is to start reading those college catalogs. College guidebooks, admissions offices, and guidance counselors should have this information as well.

As to which tests you should take, the answer is simple:

1.  those Subject Tests that you will do well on
2.  the tests that the colleges you are applying to may require you to take

The best possible situation, of course, is when the two overlap.

Some colleges have specific requirements; others do not. Again, start asking questions before you start taking tests. Once you find out which tests are required, if any, part of your decision making is done. The next step is to find out which of the tests will highlight your particular strengths.

Possibilities range from math, English literature, U.S. or world history, biology, chemistry, and physics to a variety of foreign languages.

As to when you should take the tests, schedule them as close as possible to your school's corresponding academic calendar. If you plan to take the SAT Chemistry Subject Test, for example, and you are currently taking chemistry in high school, don't postpone the test until next year.

## When Are the SAT Subject Tests Offered?

In general, you can take from one to three Subject Tests per test date in October, November, December, January, May, and June at test sites across the country. Not all subjects are offered at each administration, so check the dates carefully. The College Board's website has tons of helpful information about all of the SAT subject tests: sat.collegeboard.org/about-tests/sat-subject-tests

## How Do I Register for the Tests?

To register by mail, pick up *The Paper Registration Guide for the SAT and SAT Subject Tests* at your guidance counselor's office. You can also register at the College Board website at www.collegeboard.com. This site contains other useful information such as the test dates and fees. If you have questions, you can talk to a representative at the College Board by calling 1-866-756-7346.

You may have your scores sent to you, to your school, and to four colleges of your choice. Additional reports will be sent to additional colleges for—you guessed it—additional money. Scores are made available to students via the College Board's website. To find out about the timeline of when scores are made available, please visit sat.collegeboard.org/scores.

## Have You Heard About Fee-Waiver?

Are you a lower-income student whose family is unable to afford these test fees? Fear not. You may qualify for a fee waiver. Your high school counselor or an authorized community-based organization can give you a waiver if you qualify. Fee waivers can be used for the SAT and SAT Subject Tests. More information and the requirements for qualification can be found at sat.collegeboard.org/register/sat-fee-waivers.

## A Couple of Words About Score Choice™

The good news about the SAT Subject Test is that you can choose which test scores you want colleges to see. Why is this such good news? Well, if you take more than one SAT Subject Test on a given test date, you'll be able to choose which tests from that date you'd like to submit to colleges. So if, for example, you take the French test followed by the chemistry test, but don't think the chemistry test went very well, you can simply opt out of having that chemistry score sent to your schools.

Score Choice is optional for students. This means that you aren't required to opt in and actively choose which specific scores you would like sent to colleges. If you decide not to use the score reporting, then all of the scores on file will automatically be sent when you request score reports. You should feel fine about sending along all of your scores, since most colleges consider a student's best score.

For more information about score reporting options, go to the College Board website at www.collegeboard.com.

## What's a Good Score?

That's hard to say, exactly. A good score is one that fits in the range of scores the college of your choice usually looks for or accepts. However, if your score falls below the normal score range for Podunk University, that doesn't mean you won't get into Podunk University. Schools are usually fairly flexible in what they are willing to look at as a "good" score for a particular student.

Along with your score, you will also receive a percentile rank. That number tells you how you fit in with the other test takers. In other words, a percentile rank of 60 means that 40 percent of the test takers scored above you and 60 percent scored below you.

## What Is The Princeton Review?

The Princeton Review is a test-preparation company founded in New York City. We have branches across the country and abroad. We've developed the techniques you'll find in our books, courses, and online resources by analyzing actual exams and testing the effectiveness of those techniques with our students. What makes our techniques unique is that we base our principles on the same ones used by the people who write the tests. We don't want you to waste your time with superfluous information; we'll give you just the information you'll need to get great score improvements. You'll learn to recognize and comprehend the relatively small amount of information that's actually tested. You'll also learn to avoid common traps, to think like the test writers, to find answers to questions you're unsure of, and to budget your time effectively.

You need to do only two things: trust the techniques, and practice, practice, practice.

The College Board publishes a book called *The Official Study Guide for all SAT Subject Tests* with practice exams for all 20 SAT subjects offered. You can also go to the College Board website for more information and practice questions. After you have worked through the review chapters and completed the practice tests in this book, try out your new skills on real SAT Subject Test questions.

## What Makes This Book Different?

Most prep books for foreign language tests are written by academics who ramble on about the subtleties of the syntax of their chosen language. Their cups runneth over with more rules about grammar than you could ever absorb in a limited period of time. Most of all, they take more interest in teaching you French with a capital F than in preparing you for the particular challenges of this test. Rather than waste your time rehashing every tedious rule of grammar, we'll cover only those points needed to get you a good score on the test. We want you to study effectively.

Some prep books can harm you more than help you by misleading you about the types of questions or by giving you so much to review that you don't know where to begin or what's most important. In more than twenty years of test-prep experience, we've learned what you truly need to know to score your best.

## What Is the SAT French Subject Test?

You can choose to take one of the two French Subject Tests: French or French with Listening. While the French Subject Test is generally offered on every SAT Subject Test date (except November), French with Listening is given only in November. It has an additional audio portion, which evaluates your ability to comprehend spoken French. You listen to a recording and answer multiple-choice questions. If you intend to continue your French language study, this is useful for placement purposes. You are not tested on your speaking or writing ability on either of these tests.

## Will Slang or Casual Expressions Be Included on the Test?

Only authentic and widely accepted French language is used on the test. The SAT French is testing what should have been taught in a minimum of two years of regular French study in high school. Of course, the more you study, the better your scores will be.

## What Does It Test?

The SAT French tests vocabulary, reading comprehension, and a few points of grammar. A strong vocabulary will help you score well on the Vocabulary and Reading Comprehension sections. Our review groups words by category for easier recall and gives you tips for learning vocabulary.

As you probably know, French grammar is complex, but the SAT French Subject Test requires you to know only a small portion of all grammar. You do not need to know spelling, where the accents go, or correct word order in a sentence. You don't need to know how to conjugate the *passé simple* or the imperfect of the subjunctive. We'll review only those points of grammar that serve you best on the test.

## Now for the Good News

In the scheme of standardized tests, the SAT French Test isn't all that bad. Any standardized test provides you with a wealth of opportunity. Wouldn't you rather take a test in which you can use the Process of Elimination and guessing techniques than walk into a room and speak to a French person? By using an approach that has been developed over the years at The Princeton Review, you'll have the confidence and the ability to ace the SAT French Subject Test.

## How Is the SAT French Subject Test Scored?

The scoring system for the SAT French Test is similar to that for the SAT. You are given a raw score based on the number of questions you got right minus one-third of a point for every wrong answer. The raw score is then converted to a scaled score ranging from 200 to 800.

## How Will I Improve My Score?

Unfortunately, reading through this book may not be enough. It is important that you apply our techniques during the practice sections so that our approach will be second nature when you take the actual test.

Read one section of the book at a time and immediately apply what you have learned to the practice section that follows it. Then, carefully read through the explanations, looking for patterns in the mistakes that you made. If you notice that one type of question or topic is giving you trouble, go back and review the relevant section. Finally, before taking the diagnostic tests at the back of the book, review both the general test-taking strategies and the specific question strategies. Again, after taking the test, notice where your mistakes were, and use that information to adjust your pacing and intensify your review.

This book is designed to help you focus on those points that will help you score higher. It assumes that you have a basic French vocabulary and a rough grasp of grammar. The grammar section highlights the rules that are actually tested, giving you a concise explanation of each rule and examples of test questions. If you are someone who likes detailed explanations, you may want to have your school grammar book handy to use alongside this review book.

For more information visit www.PrincetonReview.com.

You can't master all of the French language in a few weeks or even a month. Focus on the vocabulary and grammar that helps you on the test.

Your SAT French score may be used to place you into the appropriate level of French class in college. If you score well, you may be able to take fewer semesters of language class. If you score really well, you may be exempted from the language requirement completely.

Although this book can be used alone, you may find it handy to have a French/English dictionary and a grammar book available as references while you read through the text. Don't use them on the practice tests, though!

## OVERALL STRUCTURE OF THE TEST

The SAT French Subject Test consists of four types of multiple-choice questions. You are free to work on the sections or questions in any order that you choose. You will have 60 minutes to answer 85 questions.

The layout of each test will look something like this:

- Part A—Vocabulary Completions
  (approximately 20–26 questions)
- Part B—Grammar Blanks
  (approximately 15–20 questions)
- Part C—Paragraph Blanks
  (approximately 12–20 questions)
- Part D—Reading Comprehension
  (approximately 27 questions)

The exact breakdown of questions varies from test to test. The list above gives you the approximate number of each type of question.

If Reading Comprehension contains "schedules and tickets" questions as well as traditional passages, then Reading Comprehension will have more questions and Grammar will have slightly fewer.

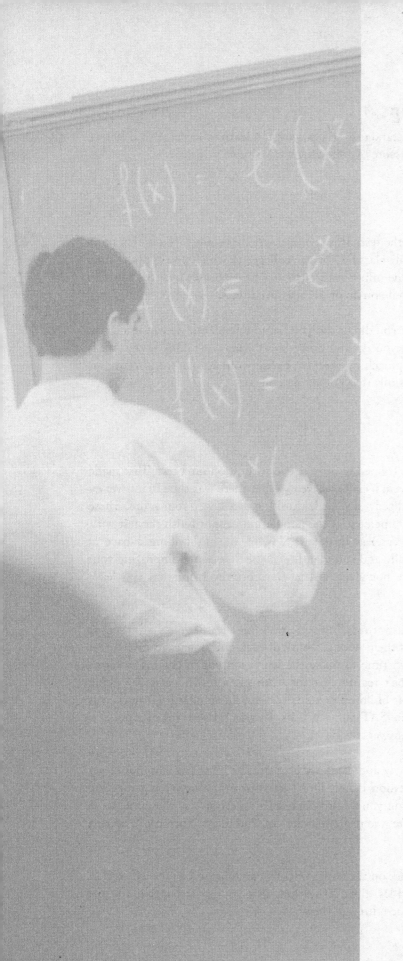

# Chapter 2
# General Strategy

In this chapter, we'll discuss the best way for you to approach the SAT French Subject Test. Pacing, Process of Elimination, and knowing when or whether to guess are all important factors that can determine how many points you accumulate as you work. You will also get a first look at the structure of the exam so you can plan your study time accordingly. Good luck!

# HOW TO IMPROVE

As on any multiple-choice standardized test, you can learn to leverage your knowledge into the best possible score by following a few simple principles.

## Attitude

Do not be intimidated by the test! This is only a test that stamps you with a number so that you can be easily classified by the colleges to which you apply. It measures some vocabulary, some minor rules such as which phrases take the subjunctive, and, above all, how well you do on standardized tests.

We can't make up for what you did or didn't learn in school, but we can teach you to make the most of what you do know and boost your test-taking savvy. We'll teach you new ways of approaching the test: pacing yourself, spotting wrong answers, and using guessing skills that put you in control.

## Pacing

Standardized tests aren't like school tests. They are actually designed so that hardly anyone can finish all the questions. Don't stress about answering every question or getting through the entire test.

In school, most of us were trained to answer every question on a test. That made sense because those tests were usually written so that there was time to answer every question. On standardized tests, such thinking can lower your score. These tests are designed so that 99 percent of the population cannot finish the test without rushing and making careless mistakes. Slowing down—finding a pace at which you can work carefully and confidently—is the first step to improving your score. Remember: You are not given a negative score on a question you leave unanswered.

There is no advantage to answering all the questions on a test if you answer so hurriedly that you get most of them wrong. Think of each question as an investment in your score. Take enough time to make the work you put in pay off in terms of points. Most people don't realize that they can get a terrific score by doing fewer questions. While this philosophy holds true for all standardized tests, it is especially important for the SAT Subject Tests, in which one-third of a point is deducted for each wrong answer.

One caution: Working slowly and carefully is great. Spending five minutes to get an answer on a single question is not. Don't let your pride keep you struggling with a question that's giving you a hard time; each question has the same value. Do what you can, eliminate wrong answer choices, and guess. Then move on to a new question.

You'll have one hour to work on the entire test. You are not timed on each section. That means you can spend less time on sections that you are stronger in, or just move at a steady, careful pace through the whole test.

## Work for Accuracy, Not for Speed

The scoring system used by the College Board rewards you for slowing down. It is better to do fewer questions well than to do many questions badly.

The following guide tells you approximately how many questions you have to answer to get a particular score. (This is the approximate number you should answer—not counting guesses—making no more than five errors.) Keep in mind that the scale changes each year, depending on the difficulty of the exam.

| To get this score: | Answer this many questions (out of 85): |
| --- | --- |
| 500 | 25 |
| 550 | 35 |
| 600 | 45 |
| 650 | 55 |
| 700 | 65 |
| 750 | 75 |
| 800 | 85 |

So, to get a 600 you have to answer barely half of the test. You can skip the questions that give you the most trouble.

You could skip as many as 20 questions and still score a 700.

As you do each practice section, you can check your pacing by comparing the number you got right with the number you got wrong. If you made more than two careless errors in that section (not counting guesses), you may want to slow down and attempt fewer questions on the practice test.

## Which Ones Should You Skip?

On Parts A and B, the questions are arranged roughly in order of increasing difficulty, so unless you are aiming for more than a 600, you may skip the last third of each part. On Parts C and D, there is no clear order of difficulty. Skip questions you don't like and spend time on those you do.

You don't have to answer the same proportion of questions on each part. For most people, reading comprehension is the most difficult and vocabulary is the easiest. If that's true for you, do extra vocabulary and fewer reading-comprehension questions.

Tailor your pacing strategy to your strengths and weaknesses. If your reading ability is strong and your grammar is weak, pace yourself accordingly.

## Process of Elimination

No matter how good you are at French, you may still come across a question or two that will stump you. What can you do? Look for obviously incorrect answers, and get rid of them. It is often easier to find three wrong answers than it is to find one right one. If the sentence completion has something to do with going to the beach, an answer choice that means "pincushion" is probably not what you're looking for. The College Board also has some favorite ways to trap test takers who aren't completely sure of themselves. Once you know how they trick you, you're protected from falling into that trap and you're one answer choice closer to the correct one. On some occasions, you may even be able to eliminate all but the correct choice.

## Make Only Smart Guesses

Eliminate as many of the wrong answer choices as possible, then guess. The way the test is scored, you get one point for each right answer and you lose only a fraction of a point for the wrong answers. You should skip the question if you really have no clue. However, if you can eliminate even one or two answer choices, it's to your advantage to guess. If you're down to two choices and can't decide, guess and move on to the next question.

# Part II
# Content Review and Strategies

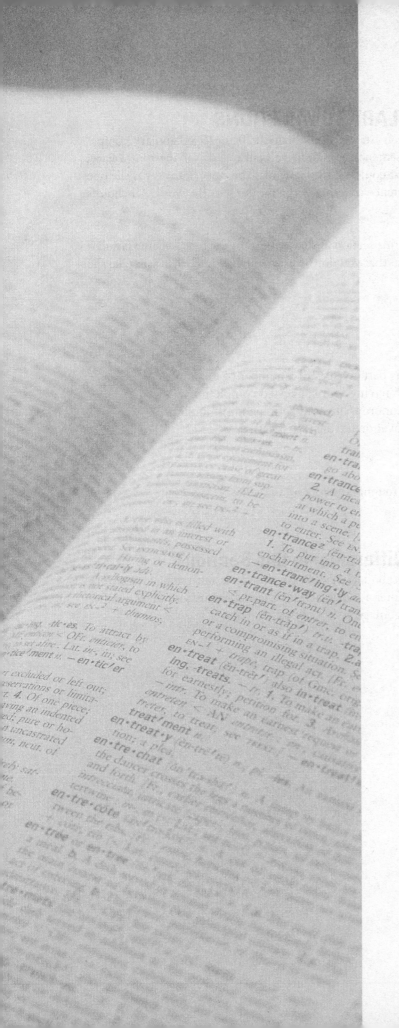

# Chapter 3
# Vocabulary

This chapter gives you several techniques to boost your score on Part A of the SAT French Subject Test. First, get acquainted with the format and structure of the vocabulary section of the test. If you understand how the test writers think, you can get a question right even if you don't know the answer. Then you'll learn additional strategies that will get you more points—tactics to use depending on how well you understand the question. What do you do if you are not sure of the answer? What if you do not know the meaning of the sentence? What if you do not know all the words in the answer choices? Just follow the simple steps we give you, and you'll be ready to handle any of these situations.

## PART A: VOCABULARY COMPLETIONS

The first part of the test consists of approximately 20 to 26 vocabulary completions. Each question is a sentence containing a blank. Each of the four answer choices provides a word that could fill in the blank. The correct answer is the one that best completes the sentence in terms of the meaning of the word. All choices will be grammatically correct.

Here are the directions for this section as they appear on the test. Become familiar with these directions now so that you don't waste valuable time when you take the test.

### Part A

> **Directions:** This part consists of a number of incomplete statements, each having four suggested completions. Select the most appropriate completion and fill in the corresponding oval on the answer sheet.

If your vocabulary needs work, short, frequent study sessions will help you more than long, infrequent ones. Your brain will be able to absorb only a small amount of information at a time. Ten minutes a day between now and the test will make a big difference.

The questions are arranged roughly in order of difficulty.

## What Makes the Difference in this Section?

Vocabulary, vocabulary, vocabulary. If your vocabulary is not strong, start working on it right away. In Chapter 4, Vocabulary Review, there are several techniques designed to boost your vocabulary.

# DRILL 1

Test your vocabulary by writing the English translations of the following words. Answers can be found in Part III.

| | |
|---|---|
| une usine | factory |
| la honte | shame |
| l'œuvre | work |
| en vouloir à | to be angry at |
| mou | soft |
| taquiner | _____ |
| la foule | _____ |
| ramasser | _____ |
| soutenir | _____ |
| repasser | _____ |
| se méfier de | _____ |
| se débarrasser de | _____ |

If you missed more than three of the words, you may need to give vocabulary work extra attention (Chapter 4).

# IF YOU KNOW THE WORDS

## Fill in Your Own Word

As you read through the sentence, fill in your own word in English **before you look** at the answer choices. Cover the answer choices with your hand, if need be.

> Le film était tellement amusant qu'elle . . . sans cesse.

If something is funny, what does someone do?

Now let's look at the answer choices and see which one is closest to the English answer you decided on:

>   (A)  dansait
>   (B)  mangeait
>   (C)  riait
>   (D)  lisait

If you thought of the word "laughed" or "smiled," you can eliminate *dansait*, which means "danced," *mangeait*, which means "ate," and *lisait*, which means "read." The correct answer is *riait*, "laughed."

If you understand most of the words in the question, you'll have no problem filling in the blank.

Cover the answer choices and fill in a word for the following examples.

> Jean-Pierre a mal . . . parce qu'il a trop mangé.
>
>   (A)  à l'oreille
>   (B)  au ventre
>   (C)  aux genoux
>   (D)  à la tête

If someone ate too much, he would probably have a pain in the "belly." You could then eliminate (A), which means "the ear," (C), which means "the knees," and (D), which means "the head." Choice (B), meaning "the abdomen," is the correct answer.

> La banque se trouve . . . le supermarché et la poste.
>
>   (A)  dans
>   (B)  sur
>   (C)  pendant
>   (D)  entre

The word in the blank should give the position of the bank in relationship to the supermarket and the post office: "between" or "near." You can eliminate (A), which means "inside," (B), which means "on," and (C), which means "during." Choice (D), which means "between," is the correct answer.

## Watch Out for Trap Answers

Don't immediately pick the first word that seems right. Look at all the answer choices, and leave in only those that might work. Then carefully compare the remaining choices before selecting an answer.

> Si tu n'as pas assez d'argent pour acheter le livre,
> tu peux le trouver à . . .

(A) la librairie
(B) l'épicerie
(C) la bibliothèque
(D) la papeterie

If you don't have enough money to buy a book, you will probably go to a "library." If you know the vocabulary, you might immediately identify the right answer. If not, eliminate (B), which means "grocery store," and (D), which means "stationery store." Is the answer *librairie* or *bibliothèque?* Which means "library?" The answer in this case is the less obvious one: (C), *bibliothèque. Librairie* means "bookstore." See page 59 for "Common Mix-Ups."

On average, each Part A section contains one question that tests your knowledge of words for body parts and one question that tests the words for different types of stores.

# IF YOU DON'T KNOW ALL THE ANSWER CHOICES

Sometimes you'll be able to fill in a word, but you won't be sure which answer choice matches the word you picked. The following guessing techniques will improve your odds of picking the correct answer.

## Use Process of Elimination (POE)

First, clear out the obviously wrong options. Eliminate answer choices that you are sure do not match the word you chose. With the remaining choices, try to narrow down what each means.

## Use Your English

Although it is your knowledge of French that is being tested, your own native language can often help you. Many English words are derived from French, so it makes sense that some words are nearly identical in both languages (but, again, watch out for those traps). How hard is it to guess what *régulier* means? *Transporter? Bière?*

# DRILL 2

Decide what English words the following French words remind you of. Answers can be found in Part III.

évaluer      _____

sacré        _____

retarder     _____

fréquenter   _____

nombre       _____

assurer      _____

raison       _____

plante       _____

attraper     _____

servir       _____

content      _____

accord       _____

cru          _____

Using English can help you make an educated guess about the meaning of a word. Based on that guess, you can decide to keep the word or eliminate it, narrowing the field of choices and improving your odds. Don't automatically pick the first word that reminds you of the English word you are looking for.

Use this technique with caution on hard questions. On difficult questions (especially the last five questions), use this technique only to eliminate wrong choices, not to pick the right answer. On tough questions, if an answer choice reminds you strongly of the word you're looking for in English, it's practically guaranteed that it's a trap answer.

On easy questions (the first third of the section), the right answer will not be a tough vocabulary word. On hard questions (the final third), the right answer will not be the answer that reminds you of the word in English that you are looking for.

27. ------- des étudiants sortant de l'école a rompu le
     silence du quartier.

   (A) Le martelage
   (B) La chatière
   (C) Le ramassage
   (D) Le bavardage

This is a tough question. If you understand the sentence ("The _____ of the students leaving school broke the silence in the neighborhood."), you know you're looking for a word that means noise, talk, or chatter. Which answer is a trap?

Choice (B) looks like the English word "chatter." Since this is a hard question (from the final third), you know it's a trap. *La chatière* actually means "the cat/pet door." The correct answer is (D), which means "the chatting." (A) means "the hammering" (*un marteau* is a hammer), and (C) means "the gathering." On difficult questions, don't pick the answer that reminds you of the word you're looking for in English.

On hard questions, be wary of trap answers but don't psych yourself out! If you know the meaning of all the words, the right answer is still the right answer. Don't cross off the right answer because you're afraid it's too "obvious." Trap answers have a specific feel to them.

Find as many opportunities as possible to hear and speak French. Check your TV or radio guides for programs in French, watch French movies, and go to websites in French, such as
www.tv5.fr
www.rfi.fr
www.lemonde.fr

## Look for Easier Versions of Words

On difficult questions (or if your vocabulary isn't very strong), you can sometimes figure out an easier version of the answer choices. For example, in the verb *feuilleter* you may see the word *feuille*, meaning "leaf" or "sheet of paper." Could there be a verb meaning "to leaf"? Yes, just as in English, you can "leaf" through a book.

What easier words do you see in the following words?

prochainement  _____

emporter  _____

parapluie  _____

retarder  _____

Well? In *prochainement,* you probably saw *prochain,* which means "next," so *prochainement* probably has something to do with being next. (It means "in a short while" or "coming up next.") You probably see *porter,* which means "to carry," in *emporter,* so you might be able to guess that *emporter* has a similar meaning. It means "to carry away." And what about *parapluie*? Recognize the word *pluie,* "rain"? So *parapluie* is likely to be "umbrella." *Retarder* has the word *tard,* or "late," in it, so it's a safe bet that *retarder* means "to slow or delay."

## Avoid Look-Alike Answers

The College Board sometimes tries to trick you by providing answers that look like either the correct answer or a word that appeared in the sentence.

Je dois réparer ma montre; elle ne . . . plus.

(A) casse
(B) montre
(C) donne
(D) marche

If something needs to be fixed, what doesn't it do anymore? Most likely, it doesn't work. Which answer choice means "to work"? Answer choice (B) is a look-alike trap here. *Montre,* meaning "show," is identical to the word *montre,* meaning "wristwatch," in the sentence. It's a trap! Eliminate it. The correct answer is (D) *marche.* The verb *marcher* used with an inanimate object means "to work or function correctly."

# IF YOU DON'T UNDERSTAND THE SENTENCE

## Word Association

Even if you're shaky on the exact meaning of the sentence, you can still make an educated guess for the answer. Go through the words in the sentence that you do know and see if any of the answer choices are in some way associated with those words.

You often don't need the whole sentence to figure out what word you're looking for. Usually one or two key words in the sentence point to the answer.

# DRILL 3

For the following incomplete questions, pick the answer choice that makes the most sense given the words that are shown.

Answers can be found in Part III.

1. xxxxxx xxxxxxxx *légumes* xxxx xxxxx . . .
   vegetables

   (A) cheminée
   (B) jardin
   (C) gazon
   (D) quartier

2. xxxx xxxxxxx x *tombé* xxx xxxx . . . fallen

   (A) envolée
   (B) échappée
   (C) cassée
   (D) attrapée

3. xx x xxx xxxxx *chaises* xxxx . . . xxxx xx xxxxx.
   chairs

   (A) assommer
   (B) s'asseoir
   (C) assurer
   (D) associer

4. xxxx *ne se sent pas bien* xxxxx xxx . . . doesn't
   feel well

   (A) une fièvre
   (B) une armoire
   (C) un verger
   (D) une annonce

5. xxxx xxxxxxxxx xxxxx *mangé* xxx xxx . . .
   eaten

   (A) soutenir
   (B) emporter
   (C) avaler
   (D) évaluer

# Comprehensive Drill

Answers can be found in Part III.

## Part A

**Directions:** This part consists of a number of incomplete statements, each having four suggested completions. Select the most appropriate completion and fill in the corresponding oval on the answer sheet.

1. Il fait froid dehors. Est-ce que toutes les . . . sont fermées?

   (A) chambres
   (B) cheminées
   (C) fenêtres
   (D) notes

2. Ne fais pas de bruit; les enfants sont . . .

   (A) venus
   (B) endormis
   (C) partis
   (D) tristes

3. Est-ce que ces fleurs sont de votre . . . ?

   (A) peinture
   (B) garage
   (C) jardin
   (D) verger

4. Ce manteau n'a pas de . . . où mettre mon porte-monnaie.

   (A) manches
   (B) portes
   (C) poches
   (D) monnaie

5. Jeanne s'est réveillée . . . pour voir le lever du soleil.

   (A) bas
   (B) haut
   (C) tard
   (D) tôt

6. Le train est parti . . . à midi.

   (A) du garage
   (B) du toit
   (C) de l'histoire
   (D) de la gare

7. Au repas du dimanche, nous mangeons un . . . avec des pommes de terre.

   (A) rôti
   (B) ruban
   (C) régime
   (D) rôle

8. Les tartes qui sont vendues dans cette . . . sont délicieuses.

   (A) pâtisserie
   (B) pharmacie
   (C) épicerie
   (D) librairie

9. Tu peux te laver maintenant. La salle de bains est . . .

   (A) gratuite
   (B) libre
   (C) livrée
   (D) seule

10. Mon . . . pour la classe est de traduire un poème de Rimbaud.

    (A) destin
    (B) composition
    (C) droit
    (D) devoir

11. Le bruit dans un club peut être tellement fort qu'on a mal . . .

(A) aux oreilles
(B) aux orteils
(C) à l'orgueil
(D) à la gorge

12. La lune est si . . . que je ne peux pas imaginer que l'homme y soit allé.

(A) longue
(B) fade
(C) loin
(D) immense

13. Ce n'est pas nécessaire de sortir la poubelle; Jean l'a . . . fait.

(A) hier
(B) ce matin
(C) déjà
(D) d'un côté

14. Nous passerons Noël avec mes grands-parents . . .

(A) cet été
(B) cet automne
(C) cet hiver
(D) ce printemps

15. Vous avez déjà fait vos devoirs? Cela . . .

(A) m'admet
(B) me fait mal
(C) me trompe
(D) m'étonne

16. N'avez-vous pas . . . d'avoir fait cette bêtise?

(A) courage
(B) joie
(C) hâte
(D) honte

17. Ce tissu est . . . comme la peau d'un bébé.

(A) mouillé
(B) nu
(C) doux
(D) cru

18. Le renard a . . . aux chasseurs.

(A) ramassé
(B) enfui
(C) échappé
(D) couru

19. Le film commence à 8 heures exactement; soyez . . .

(A) à l'heure
(B) au courant
(C) au loin
(D) à présent

20. Il y a trop de monde ici; je préfère des cafés moins . . .

(A) doués
(B) chargés
(C) tranquilles
(D) fréquentés

21. Il n'y a pas assez de preuves pour . . . cet homme.

(A) indiquer
(B) inquiéter
(C) insinuer
(D) inculper

22. Mon frère est . . . ; il ne veut jamais m'aider à nettoyer la cuisine.

(A) serviable
(B) paresseux
(C) redoutable
(D) affolé

23. Le vase que j'ai laissé tomber s'est . . .

    (A) perdu
    (B) tricoté
    (C) évanoui
    (D) brisé

24. Vous pouvez trouver la robe de mariée de votre grand-mère si vous cherchez dans . . .

    (A) le plancher
    (B) le grenier
    (C) l'atelier
    (D) le magasin

25. Elle s'est débarrassée de ses vêtements . . .

    (A) âgés
    (B) déprimés
    (C) abîmés
    (D) achetés

26. Diane s'est coupé les . . . pour être plus à la mode.

    (A) chevaux
    (B) chiffres
    (C) cheveux
    (D) chemins

27. Pour établir la validité de sa théorie, l'homme de science a fait . . .

    (A) un échec
    (B) une expérience
    (C) un résumé
    (D) un résultat

# Summary

To increase your score, keep the following tips in mind.

- o  If you know all the words in the sentence
  - • eliminate obviously wrong answer choices
  - • examine remaining choices (to avoid obvious traps)
  - • pick your answer

- o  If you are not sure of the meaning of the sentence
  - • use word association
  - • read the question again, and see if there are any obvious traps

- o  If you do not know all of the answer choices
  - • use your English to eliminate wrong answers
  - • try to figure out the roots of the words

- o  Guess after you have eliminated as many obviously wrong answers as possible.

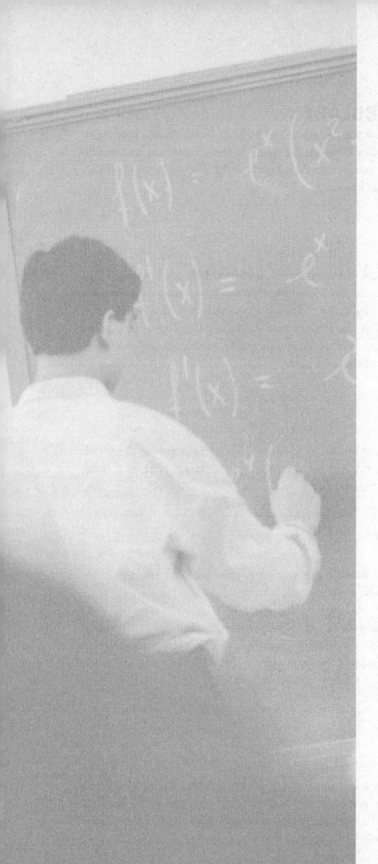

# Chapter 4
# Vocabulary Review

At this level, your basic French vocabulary should be good. The more French you read, the better you will acquire new words and feel comfortable with what you already know. The following vocabulary list should help you review. It organizes words into logical categories. This will make memorizing them easier. Look through each category and concentrate on the words you don't know or words that seem to be cognates but in fact have very different meanings.

## BOOST YOUR VOCABULARY

If you really want to imprint new vocabulary words on your brain, passive reading is not enough. Critical reading with a dictionary at hand, as well as listening and watching French media, will increase your vocabulary significantly. Try one or more of the following techniques to help your learning.

### Flashcards

Put the French word on one side, the English on the other. If you want to get fancy, color-code by category or make up a symbol. This way, you can mix up words in any order and regroup them in many different ways, such as where, when, and how the words can be used. On the French side, include part of speech, gender, and the word used in a sentence. Whenever you have a few minutes, pull out your cards and test yourself. Think of this as a game.

### Mnemonics

If it works for you, think of a funny image or sound that corresponds to the word. The more outrageous, the easier it will be to remember. Make up your own mnemonics and add them to your flashcards.

### Posters

Make a list of words and definitions and hang it on your wall. As you go about your day, glance at the poster and review a few words.

These are only a few of the ways you can work on your vocabulary. Anything you do to make it more creative or colorful (literally—use colored pens, colored index cards, stickers, or markers) will increase your ability to learn and remember vocabulary.

**Vocabulary**
Color-code your vocabulary list! Use three different highlighters to keep track of words you know, words you sort of know, and words you've never seen before. Assign a different color to each category so you know which words you need to work on.

## VOCABULARY LIST

This section will help you review key vocabulary words. It is not the only vocabulary you need to know for the test, however. You will find suggestions for how to continue enriching your vocabulary. Pay particular attention to the commonly mixed-up words and false cognates.

## Le Calendrier et le Temps
## Une Année

| | |
|---|---|
| *un an* | a year (always used for age) |
| *une décennie* | a decade |
| *une année* | a year (as in *l'année dernière*, last year) |
| *un mois* | a month |
| *une semaine* | a week |
| *un jour* | a day |
| *une journée* | a day (as in *toute la journée*, all day long) |
| *un siècle* | a century |
| *un calendrier* | a calendar |
| *un horaire* | a schedule |

## The Calendar and the Time
## A Year

## Un Jour

| | |
|---|---|
| *le matin* | the morning |
| *la matinée* | the morning (as in *toute la matinee*) |
| *l'après-midi (m or f)* | the afternoon |
| *le soir* | the evening |
| *la soirée* | the evening |
| *la nuit* | the night |
| *l'aube (f)* | daybreak |
| *l'aurore (f)* | dawn |
| *le crépuscule* | twilight |
| *le lever du soleil* | the sunrise |
| *le coucher du soleil* | the sunset |
| *un jour férié* | a holiday |
| *un jour de congé* | a day off |
| *faire la grasse matinée* | to sleep late |

## A Day

## Une Heure

| | |
|---|---|
| *minuit* | midnight |
| *midi* | noon |
| *une montre* | a watch |
| *un réveil* | an alarm clock |
| *une horloge, une pendule* | a clock |
| *un minuteur* | a timer (in the kitchen) |
| *un chronomètre* | a stop watch |

## An Hour

### *Un An* vs. *Une Année*
What's the difference between *un an* and *une année*? It's subtle. *Un an* is a unit of time. For example, "*J'ai passé deux ans à Paris.*" *Une année* is used when describing not the unit, but the full span of time. For example, "*l'année que j'ai passée en France….*" The same concept is used for *un matin—une matinée, un soir—une soirée, un jour—une journée.*

### *Lundi* vs. *Le Lundi*
Observe what happens when you use the definite article *le*. *Lundi* means "Monday." *Le lundi* means "on Mondays." Also, notice the following expressions: *Tous les lundis* means "every Monday." *Lundi en huit* means "a week from Monday." (Monday to Monday is eight days.)

## Les Expressions de Temps — Expressions of Time

| | |
|---|---|
| *être à l'heure* | to be on time |
| *être en retard* | to be late |
| *être en avance* | to be ahead of schedule |
| *tôt* | early |
| *tard* | late |
| *avant* | before |
| *après* | after |
| *le lendemain* | the day after |
| *hier* | yesterday |
| *désormais* | from now on / from then on |
| *pendant* | during |
| *arriver de bonne heure* | to arrive early |
| *déjà* | already |
| *bientôt* | soon |
| *prochainement* | shortly |
| *toujours* | always / still |
| *ne…pas encore* | not yet |
| *ne…jamais* | never |
| *longtemps* | for a long time |
| *régulièrement* | regularly |
| *d'habitude* | usually |
| *habituellement* | usually |
| *autrefois* | in the past |
| *parfois* | sometimes |
| *chaque jour* | each / every day |
| *se dépêcher* | to hurry |
| *se précipiter* | to rush |
| *Un instant!* | Just a moment! |
| *Ne quittez pas!* | Please hold (on)! |

## Les Saisons (f) — Seasons

| | |
|---|---|
| *le printemps* | spring |
| *l'été (m)* | summer |
| *l'automne (m)* | autumn, fall |
| *l'hiver (m)* | winter |

# La Nature et le Temps

# Nature and the Weather

| | |
|---|---|
| *la météo* | the weather forecast |
| *le soleil* | the sun, the sunshine |
| *être bronzé* | to be tanned |
| *prendre un coup de soleil* | to get sunburnt |
| *attraper une insolation* | to get sunstroke |
| *Quel temps fait-il?* | What's the weather like? |
| *il fait beau* | the weather is nice |
| *il fait chaud* | it is hot |
| *avoir chaud* | to be hot |
| *par beau temps* | in good weather |
| *le nuage* | the cloud |
| *la pluie* | the rain |
| *il pleut / pleuvoir* | it is raining / to rain |
| *une averse* | a shower |
| *il pleut des cordes* | it's raining hard |
| *être trempé(e)* | to be soaked |
| *être mouillé(e)* | to be wet |
| *il fait mauvais* | the weather is bad |
| *par mauvais temps* | in bad weather |
| *la neige* | the snow |
| *la glace* | the ice |
| *il neige* | it is snowing |
| *il fait froid* | it is cold |
| *avoir froid* | to be cold |
| *un ciel couvert* | an overcast sky |
| *un orage* | a thunderstorm |
| *il y a des éclairs* | there is lightning |
| *le tonnerre* | thunder |
| *le brouillard* | the fog |
| *la brume* | light fog / a mist |
| *le vent* | the wind |
| *une tempête* | a storm |
| *un ouragan* | a hurricane |
| *la rosée du matin* | the morning dew |
| *une rafale de vent* | a gust of wind |
| *une bourrasque* | a squall |

***Pleurer* vs. *Pleuvoir***

A common mistake is to mix up *pleurer* (to cry) and *pleuvoir* (to rain).

| | |
|---|---|
| *briller* | to shine |
| *souffler* | to blow |
| *il fait noir / sombre* | it is dark |
| *prédire* | to predict |

## Le Plein Air — The Outdoors

| | |
|---|---|
| *dehors* | outside |
| *un arbre* | a tree |
| *un buisson* | a bush |
| *l'écorce d'un arbre* | the bark |
| *une feuille* | a leaf |
| *une prairie* | a meadow |
| *un champ* | a field |
| *l'herbe (f)* | grass |
| *le gazon / la pelouse* | the lawn |
| *une rivière* | a river |
| *un fleuve* | a river flowing into the sea |
| *la mer* | the sea |
| *une étoile* | a star |
| *la lune* | the moon |
| *un verger* | an orchard |
| *le jardin* | the garden |
| *une fleur* | a flower |
| *la poussière* | the dust |
| *récolter* | to harvest |
| *ramasser* | to gather, to pick up |
| *se promener / faire une promenade* | to take a walk |
| *prendre l'air* | to get some fresh air, to take a walk |
| *faire une randonnée* | to go hiking |
| *tondre la pelouse* | to mow the lawn |

## La Maison — The Home

| | |
|---|---|
| *un toit* | a roof |
| *un plafond* | a ceiling |
| *une cheminée* | a chimney, a fireplace |
| *un mur* | a wall |
| *une fenêtre* | a window |

| | |
|---|---|
| *un volet* | a shutter |
| *en haut* | upstairs |
| *en bas* | downstairs |
| *les toilettes / les WC* | the restroom (toilet) |
| *la salle de bains* | the bathroom (bath) |
| *une baignoire* | a bathtub |
| *prendre un bain* | to take a bath |
| *une douche* | a shower |
| *prendre une douche / se doucher* | to take a shower |
| *une serviette* | a towel |
| *un savon* | a bar of soap |
| *un lavabo* | a bathroom sink |
| *une glace / un miroir* | a mirror |
| *la chambre à coucher* | the bedroom |
| *un lit* | a bed |
| *une armoire* | a closet |
| *un meuble* | a piece of furniture |
| *un tiroir* | a drawer |
| *un aspirateur* | a vacuum cleaner |
| *un climatiseur* | an air conditioner |
| *un rideau* | a curtain |
| *un oreiller* | a pillow |
| *un matelas* | a mattress |
| *une couverture* | a blanket |
| *un drap* | a sheet |
| *un plancher* | a wooden floor |
| *le sol* | the floor |
| *le salon / la salle de séjour* | the living room |
| *une chaise* | a chair |
| *un divan / un canapé* | a couch |
| *un tableau* | a painting, a picture |
| *un fauteuil* | an armchair |
| *ouvrir* | to open |
| *fermer* | to close |
| *se coucher* | to go to bed |
| *s'endormir* | to fall asleep |
| *se réveiller* | to wake up |

**This Should "Cover" It**
Some common mix-ups are *les couvertures* (the blankets), *le couvert* (the table setting), and *le couvercle* (the lid).

| | |
|---|---|
| *s'allonger* | to lie down |
| *avoir sommeil* | to be sleepy |
| *se lever* | to get up |
| *s'asseoir* | to sit down |
| *la salle à manger* | the dining room |
| *la cuisine* | the kitchen |
| *un évier* | a kitchen sink |
| *un four* | an oven |
| *un appareil ménager* | an appliance |
| *un réfrigérateur* | a refrigerator |
| *une poubelle* | a garbage can |
| *un pot* | a jar |
| *une casserole* | a pan |
| *une poêle* | a frying pan |
| *une cuisinière* | a stove |
| *un cuisinier / une cuisinière* | a cook |
| *le grenier* | the attic |
| *la cave* | the cellar |
| *un coin* | a corner |
| *le sous-sol* | the basement |
| *un atelier* | a studio, a workshop |
| *le rez-de-chaussée* | the ground floor |
| *un / une concierge* | a building superintendent / a custodian |
| *une boîte à lettres* | a mail box |
| *le courrier* | the mail |
| *frotter* | to rub |
| *astiquer* | to polish |
| *balayer* | to sweep |
| *nettoyer* | to clean |
| *faire le ménage* | to do the housework |
| *faire la vaisselle* | to wash the dishes |
| *faire la cuisine* | to cook |
| *faire la poussière* | to dust |
| *ranger* | to put away |
| *monter* | to go up / to bring up |
| *descendre* | to go down / to bring down |
| *rester* | to stay |

**False Cognates**

*Un coin* means "a corner," NOT "a coin." *Une pièce de monnaie* is a coin. *Une cave* means "a cellar." *Une caverne* is a cave. *Un plat* means "a dish" (as in part of a meal). *Une assiette* is a plate.

| | |
|---|---|
| *se reposer* | to rest |
| *quitter (+ un nom)* | to leave (a place or a person) |
| *partir* | to leave |
| *bricoler* | to fix |

## En Ville (f)

| | |
|---|---|
| *un immeuble* | a building |
| *un gratte-ciel* | a skyscraper |
| *un trottoir* | a sidewalk |
| *un passant* | a passer-by |
| *une rue* | a street |
| *un rond-point* | a traffic circle |
| *une zone piétonne* | a pedestrian zone |
| *un quartier* | a neighborhood |
| *un endroit* | a place |
| *une gare* | a train station |
| *une piscine* | a swimming pool |
| *une banlieue* | a suburb |
| *habiter dans les environs de* | to live on the outskirts of |
| *habiter en banlieue* | to live in the suburbs |
| *un stade* | a stadium |
| *un théâtre* | a theater |
| *assister à un concert* | to attend a concert |
| *une foule* | a crowd |
| *la boulangerie* | the bakery |
| *un boulanger / une boulangère* | a baker |
| *une pâtisserie* | a pastry shop, a pastry |
| *un pâtissier / une pâtissière* | a pastry cook |
| *une épicerie* | a grocery store |
| *un épicier / une épicière* | a grocer |
| *une fromagerie* | a cheese store |
| *une boucherie* | a butcher shop |
| *un boucher / une bouchère* | a butcher |
| *une charcuterie* | a delicatessen |
| *un charcutier / une charcutière* | a pork butcher |
| *une papeterie* | a stationery store |

## In Town

**False Cognates**

*Rester* means "to stay," NOT "to rest." *Se reposer* means "to rest." *Quitter* means "to leave," NOT "to quit." Use *quitter* instead of *partir* when you mean it to be more permanent. Examples: *Quitter son domicile; quitter son pays; quitter l'école. Abandonner* means "to quit."

**False Cognates**

*Assister à* means "to attend," NOT "to assist." *Aider quelqu'un* means "to assist someone."

| | |
|---|---|
| une librairie | a bookstore |
| une bibliothèque | a library |
| un marché aux puces | a flea market |
| une quincaillerie | a hardware store |
| la boutique de bricolage | the do-it-yourself department |
| un tabac / un bureau de tabac | a shop selling tobacco items, stamps, newspapers |
| une banque | a bank |
| un kiosque à journaux | a newsstand |

## Faire les Courses (f) — Shopping for Food

| | |
|---|---|
| la nourriture | food |
| la recette | a recipe |
| le pain | bread |
| un croissant | a croissant |
| les pâtisseries (f) | pastries |
| une tarte | a tart |
| un gâteau | a cake |
| un chou à la crème | a cream-puff |
| un petit gâteau / un biscuit | a cookie |
| un biscuit salé | a cracker |
| un éclair | an éclair |
| les pâtes (f) | pasta |
| le riz | rice |
| le maïs | corn |
| les légumes (m) | vegetables |
| les épinards (m) | spinach |
| les haricots verts (m) | green beans |
| un oignon | an onion |
| un champignon | a mushroom |
| un poivron vert | a green pepper |
| les pommes de terre | potatoes |
| une pomme | an apple |
| les petits pois | peas |
| un avocat | an avocado |
| les fruits (m) | fruit |

**Avocado!?**
The word *avocat* means "avocado" from a word that originated in Mexico. Watch out! It also means "lawyer" from the Latin word *advocatus*. Pay attention to the context when making a vocabulary choice on the SAT French Subject Test.

| | |
|---|---|
| une fraise | a strawberry |
| une framboise | a raspberry |
| un ananas | a pineapple |
| une myrtille | a blueberry |
| une cerise | a cherry |
| une pêche | a peach |
| une poire | a pear |
| une noix | a walnut |
| une amande | an almond |
| des raisins | grapes |
| des raisins secs | raisins |
| un pamplemousse | a grapefruit |
| un concombre | a cucumber |
| le fromage | cheese |
| le beurre | butter |
| le lait | milk |
| une glace | an ice cream |
| un œuf | an egg |
| la viande | meat |
| le jambon | ham |
| le veau | veal |
| un rôti | a roast |
| une boulette de viande | a meatball |
| le sel | salt |
| le poivre | pepper |
| la confiture | jam, preserves |
| le sucre | sugar |
| l'eau | water |
| une bière | a beer |
| le vin | wine |
| livrer | to deliver |
| commander | to order |
| vendre | to sell |
| acheter | to buy |
| faire les courses | to go shopping, to run errands |
| avoir besoin de | to need |
| avoir envie de manger | to feel like eating |

| | |
|---|---|
| *l'argent (m)* | money |
| *retirer de l'argent* | to withdraw money |
| *rendre la monnaie* | to give back the change |
| *payer comptant* | to pay cash |
| *économiser* | to save money |

## Au Restaurant (m)     At the Restaurant

| | |
|---|---|
| *un restaurant* | a restaurant |
| *le repas* | the meal |
| *le déjeuner* | lunch |
| *le petit déjeuner* | breakfast |
| *le dîner* | dinner |
| *un plat* | a dish |
| *le service est compris* | service is included |
| *et comme boissons* | and for drinks? |
| *un garçon, un serveur* | a waiter |
| *une serveuse* | a waitress |
| *un pourboire* | a tip |
| *l'addition (f)* | the bill, the check |
| *le couvert* | table setting; cover charge |
| *une cuillère* | a spoon |
| *un couteau* | a knife |
| *une fourchette* | a fork |
| *une assiette* | a plate |
| *le verre* | the glass |
| *remplir* | to fill |
| *servir* | to serve |
| *se servir (de)* | to use, to help oneself (with) |
| *régler / payer l'addition* | to pay the check |
| *emporter* | to take away |
| *apporter* | to bring |
| *mettre le couvert* | to set the table |
| *débarrasser la table* | to clear the table |
| *se débarrasser de* | to get rid of |
| *fréquenter* | to go to a place frequently |
| *fréquenté* | crowded, popular |

| | |
|---|---|
| *mou / molle* | soft |
| *cru / crue* | raw |
| *cuit / cuite* | cooked |
| *bien cuit* | well-done |
| *à point* | medium rare |
| *saignant / saignante* | rare |
| *gras / grasse* | greasy, fatty |

## Le Monde du Travail

## The Working World

| | |
|---|---|
| *le chômage* | unemployment |
| *un(e) chômeur / chômeuse* | an unemployed person |
| *un ouvrier* | a worker |
| *la médecine du travail* | occupational medicine |
| *un médecin* | a physician |
| *un infirmier / une infirmière* | a nurse |
| *le droit* | law |
| *un(e) avocat(e)* | a lawyer |
| *un(e) juge* | a judge |
| *le monde artistique* | the arts |
| *un chanteur / une chanteuse* | a singer |
| *un acteur / une actrice* | an actor, an actress |
| *un(e) metteur en scène* | a director, a producer |
| *une œuvre* | a work |
| *un chef-d'œuvre* | a masterpiece |
| *le commerce / les affaires* | business |
| *une femme / un homme d'affaires* | a business woman / man |
| *un(e) comptable* | an accountant |
| *un(e) patron / patronne* | a boss |
| *un / une cadre* | an executive |
| *l'informatique (f)* | computer science |
| *un ordinateur* | a computer |
| *la facture* | the bill, the invoice |
| *l'usine (f)* | the factory |
| *l'outil (m)* | the tool |
| *embaucher* | to hire |
| *travailler* | to work |

**False Cognate**
*Travailler* means to work, not to travel.

| | |
|---|---|
| *être en grève / faire grève* | to be on strike |
| *renvoyer* | to dismiss |
| *mettre à la porte* | to fire |
| *licencier* | to lay off |

## Le Corps Humain — The Human Body

| | |
|---|---|
| *la tête* | the head |
| *la figure, le visage* | the face |
| *l'œil / les yeux (m)* | the eye / the eyes |
| *le nez* | the nose |
| *la bouche* | the mouth |
| *la lèvre* | the lip |
| *la dent* | the tooth |
| *la langue* | the tongue |
| *l'oreille (f)* | the ear |
| *le cou* | the neck |
| *l'épaule (f)* | the shoulder |
| *la poitrine* | the chest |
| *le bras* | the arm |
| *la main* | the hand |
| *le doigt* | the finger |
| *le coude* | the elbow |
| *l'ongle (m)* | the nail |
| *le poignet* | the wrist |
| *la hanche* | the hip |
| *la jambe* | the leg |
| *le genou / les genoux* | the knee / knees |
| *les cheveux* | the hair |
| *la peau* | the skin |
| *le poumon* | the lung |
| *le cœur* | the heart |
| *le ventre* | the belly |
| *le talon* | the heel |
| *le poing* | the fist |
| *un coup de poing* | a punch |
| *le rein* | the kidney |

| | |
|---|---|
| l'orteil | the toe |
| le dos | the back |
| un os | a bone |
| le sang | the blood |
| transpirer, suer | to sweat |
| respirer | to breathe |
| se faire mal à l'épaule | to hurt one's shoulder |
| avoir mal au ventre / à l'estomac | to have a stomachache |
| gros | fat |
| mince | slim, thin |
| maigre | skinny |
| être en forme | to be in shape |
| décontracté(e) | relaxed |
| muet / muette | mute |
| aveugle | blind |
| sourd(e) | deaf |
| se laver | to wash (oneself) |
| se brosser les dents | to brush one's teeth |
| se peigner | to comb one's hair |
| se coiffer | to do one's hair |
| se raser | to shave |
| se maquiller | to put makeup on |
| du rouge à lèvres | a lipstick |
| une crème | a cream |
| se sécher | to dry oneself |

**Phrase Check**
The expression *avoir mal* should be used with the proper preposition *au, à la, à l'*, or *aux* depending on the body part following the expression. *J'ai mal à la tête; il a mal aux jambes.*

## Les Vêtements (m) — Clothes

| | |
|---|---|
| au rayon femmes / hommes | in the women's / men's department |
| en solde | on sale |
| une robe | a dress |
| une robe du soir | a gown |
| une robe de chambre | a robe |
| un peignoir de bain | a bathrobe |
| une chemise de nuit | a nightgown |
| un chemisier | a woman's shirt |
| une chemise | a shirt |

| | |
|---|---|
| *un tailleur* | a woman's suit |
| *un ensemble* | a woman's suit, an outfit |
| *un costume* | a man's suit |
| *un smoking* | a tuxedo, dinner jacket |
| *une jupe* | a skirt |
| *un pull* | a sweater |
| *un col roulé* | a turtleneck sweater |
| *un manteau* | a coat |
| *un imperméable* | a raincoat |
| *un parapluie* | an umbrella |
| *une chaussure / un soulier* | a shoe |
| *une botte* | a boot |
| *une chaussette* | a sock |
| *des collants (m)* | tights |
| *un pantalon* | a pair of pants |
| *un survêtement* | a sweatsuit, a warmup suit |
| *les sous-vêtements (m. pl.)* | underwear |
| *une manche* | a sleeve |
| *un bouton* | a button |
| *une poche* | a pocket |
| *un maillot de bain* | a swimming suit / a bathing suit |
| *une ceinture* | a belt |
| *un chapeau* | a hat |
| *une casquette* | a cap |
| *un foulard* | a scarf |
| *une écharpe* | a winter scarf, a sash |
| *une cravate* | a tie |
| *un collier* | a necklace |
| *une bague* | a ring |
| *une boucle d'oreille* | an earring |
| *un fil* | a thread |
| *la soie* | silk |
| *la laine* | wool |
| *le cuir* | leather |
| *le caoutchouc* | rubber |
| *le velours côtelé* | corduroy |
| *la fourrure* | fur |

| | |
|---|---|
| *l'aiguille* | the needle |
| *la taille* | size, waist |
| *la pointure* | shoe size |
| *le cintre* | the hanger |
| *essayer* | to try on |
| *porter* | to wear |
| *mettre* | to put on |
| *froisser* | to wrinkle |
| *repasser* | to iron |
| *le repassage* | ironing |
| *déchirer* | to tear |
| *coudre* | to sew |
| *la couture* | sewing |
| *le tricot* | knitting |
| *tricoter* | to knit |
| *rétrécir* | to shrink |
| *aller bien* | to suit / to go well |
| *être à la bonne taille* | to fit |
| *avoir de l'allure* | to have style |
| *propre* | clean |
| *une tache* | a stain |
| *taché(e)* | stained |
| *à la mode* | in style, fashionable |
| *décontracté(e)* | casual |
| *démodé(e)* | out of style |
| *assorti(e) à* | matching |
| *uni(e)* | solid color |
| *à rayures* | striped |
| *imprimé(e)* | printed |
| *ecossais(e)* | plaid |
| *à fleurs* | floral |
| *à pois* | polka-dotted |
| *à carreaux* | checked |
| *délavé(e)* | faded, washed-out |

**Vocabulary**
*Allure* means "appearance," but it also means "speed" or "pace." *Il va à toute allure!* "He is going at top speed!"

**Tache vs. Tâche**
*Une tache* means "a stain." *Une tâche* means "a task."

## Les Voyages/
## Les Transports

## Travel/
## Transportation

| | |
|---|---|
| *un voyage* | a trip |
| *faire un voyage* | to go on a trip |
| *faire ses valises* | to pack one's suitcases |
| *être en vacances* | to be on vacation |
| *l'itinéraire* | the itinerary, the route |
| *la route* | the way / the road |
| *un vélo, une bicyclette* | a bicycle |
| *une voiture* | a car, a carriage, a wagon |
| *une voiture d'occasion* | a second-hand car |
| *une ceinture de sécurité* | a seatbelt |
| *une autoroute* | a highway |
| *un bouchon / un embouteillage* | a traffic jam |
| *l'heure de pointe / d'affluence* | rush hour / peak hour |
| *rouler* | to move forward, to roll, to drive |
| *conduire* | to drive |
| *doubler une voiture* | to pass a car |
| *klaxonner* | to honk |
| *interdiction de stationner* | no parking |
| *tourner à gauche / à droite* | turn left / right |
| *défense de tourner à gauche* | no left turn |
| *se garer* | to park |
| *démarrer* | to start driving |
| *un permis de conduire* | a driving license |
| *l'essence* | gas |
| *faire le plein* | to fill up the tank |
| *avoir une panne d'essence* | to run out of gas |
| *une roue* | a wheel |
| *un pneu* | a tire |
| *un pneu crevé* | a flat tire |
| *un volant* | a steering wheel |
| *un frein* | a brake |
| *un rétroviseur* | a rearview mirror |
| *un phare* | a headlight |
| *une station-service* | a gas station |

**Vocabulary**
*Un bouchon* also means "a cork." *Un embouteillage* comes from the word *une bouteille*, "a bottle."

| | |
|---|---|
| *s'arrêter* | to stop |
| *reculer* | to back up |
| *un train* | a train |
| *le chemin de fer* | the railroad |
| *une gare* | a train station |
| *un guichet* | a ticket booth |
| *demander un renseignement* | to ask for information |
| *composter* | to punch in (tickets) |
| *rater (le train)* | to miss (the train) |
| *une correspondance* | a train connection, a transfer |
| *le prochain arrêt* | the next stop |
| *un contrôleur* | a ticket inspector |
| *changer* | to transfer |
| *monter* | to get on |
| *descendre* | to get off |
| *un bateau* | a boat |
| *une voile* | a sail |
| *une bouée de sauvetage* | a life preserver |
| *un gilet de sauvetage* | a life jacket |
| *avoir le mal de mer* | to be seasick |
| *une croisière* | a cruise |
| *un avion* | a plane |
| *atterrir / se poser* | to land |
| *l'atterrissage* | the landing |
| *enregistrer les bagages* | to check in (one's luggage) |
| *décoller* | to take off |
| *le décollage* | takeoff |
| *une escale* | a stop, a stopover |
| *une aile* | a wing |
| *avoir le mal de l'air* | to feel airsick |
| *voler* | to fly |
| *un vol* | a flight |
| *l'embarquement* | boarding |
| *la douane* | customs |
| *un billet* | a ticket |
| *un aller simple* | a one-way ticket |
| *un aller-retour* | a roundtrip ticket |

| | |
|---|---|
| *une agence de voyages* | a travel agency |
| *traverser* | to cross |
| *transporter* | to transport |
| *proche* | near |
| *loin* | far |
| *le décalage horaire* | the time difference, jet lag |
| *une fusée* | a rocket |
| *complet* | full |
| *il y a de la place* | there is room |
| *une place libre* | an empty seat |
| *annulé(e)* | cancelled |

## Les Accidents et les Urgences

## Accidents and Emergencies

| | |
|---|---|
| *le dégât* | the damage |
| *la faute* | the mistake, the fault |
| *grave* | serious |
| *le témoin* | the witness |
| *une blessure* | an injury |
| *une brûlure* | a burn |
| *l'assurance (f)* | the insurance |
| *la prison* | the jail |
| *un incendie* | a wildfire, a fire |
| *un feu* | a fire |
| *une piqûre d'insecte* | a sting / an insect bite |
| *enfermer* | to lock up |
| *se couper* | to cut oneself |
| *brûler* | to burn |
| *saigner* | to bleed |
| *se casser (la jambe)* | to break (one's leg) |
| *être témoin de* | to witness |
| *assurer* | to ensure, to assure |
| *arrêter* | to stop, to arrest |
| *renverser quelqu'un* | to hit somebody (with a vehicle) |
| *soutenir* | to hold up, to support |
| *secourir, aider* | to help |
| | to save / to rescue |

**Aidez-moi!**
You call for help in French by yelling *"Au secours!"*

| | |
|---|---|
| *avoir tort* | to be wrong |
| *avoir raison* | to be right |
| *échapper à* | to escape (from) |
| *attraper* | to catch |
| *éviter* | to avoid |
| *blesser* | to injure |
| *assommer* | to knock out (a person) |
| *faire tomber* | to knock down (something) |
| *tomber* | to fall |
| *glisser* | to slip |
| *faire un plâtre / plâtrer* | to put a cast on |
| *faire un pansement* | to put a bandage / a dressing on |
| *s'étrangler* | to choke |
| *la réanimation* | resuscitation |
| *sortir indemne* | to come out unharmed |
| *heureusement* | fortunately |
| *malheureusement* | unfortunately |

## La Maladie — Illness

| | |
|---|---|
| *un rhume* | a cold |
| *une angine* | a throat infection |
| *des vertiges* | dizzy spells |
| *la nausée* | nausea |
| *une crampe* | a cramp |
| *la douleur* | pain |
| *une baisse de tension* | a drop in blood pressure |
| *la rougeole* | measles |
| *la varicelle* | chicken pox |
| *la chirurgie* | surgery |
| *la salle d'attente* | the waiting room |
| *un rendez-vous* | an appointment |
| *une ordonnance* | a prescription |
| *un comprimé* | a pill |
| *un cachet* | a tablet |
| *prendre des médicaments* | to take medicines or medication |
| *une analyse de sang* | a blood test |

| | |
|---|---|
| *avaler* | to swallow |
| *avoir mal au cœur* | to feel nauseated |
| *avoir des boutons* | to have a rash |
| *être enrhumé(e)* | to have a cold |
| *avoir de la fièvre* | to have a fever |
| *avoir la grippe* | to have the flu |
| *avoir de la tension* | to have high blood pressure |
| *avoir des palpitations* | to have palpitations |
| *s'évanouir* | to faint |
| *vomir* | to throw up |
| *éternuer* | to sneeze |
| *tousser* | to cough |
| *avoir mal à la gorge* | to have a sore throat |
| *avoir mal à la tête* | to have a headache |
| *le traitement* | the treatment |
| *soigner* | to treat |
| *se soigner* | to take care of oneself |
| *vacciner contre* | to vaccinate against |
| *faire une piqûre* | to give a shot |
| *faire une radio* | to take an X-ray |
| *aller / se porter bien...mal / mieux* | to be well / ill / better |
| *être en bonne santé / bien portant* | to be in good health |
| *être en pleine forme* | to be in top shape |
| *déprimé(e)* | depressed |
| *malade* | sick, ill |

| L'émotion (f) | Emotion |
|---|---|
| *la confiance* | confidence or trust |
| *le plaisir* | pleasure |
| *la hâte* | haste |
| *la honte* | shame |
| *la méfiance* | mistrust |
| *l'agrément (m)* | pleasure; approval |
| *un caprice* | a whim |
| *une larme* | a tear |
| *un baiser* | a kiss |
| *combler (quelqu'un)* | to gratify / to satisfy |
| *être d'accord* | to agree |
| *s'occuper (de)* | to take care of |
| *éprouver* | to feel, to experience |
| *étonner* | to astonish |
| *s'étonner de* | to be amazed by |
| *estimer* | to hold in esteem; to estimate |
| *tolérer* | to tolerate |
| *surprendre* | to surprise |
| *se méfier (de)* | to distrust |
| *faire de la peine (à)* | to hurt someone's feelings |
| *avoir de la peine* | to feel bad |
| *tromper* | to trick, to deceive |
| *se tromper* | to make a mistake |
| *changer d'avis* | to change one's mind |
| *s'amuser* | to have fun |
| *rire* | to laugh |
| *sourire* | to smile |
| *pleurer* | to cry |
| *s'embêter / s'ennuyer* | to be bored |
| *s'énerver* | to get upset |

*Avoir* and Emotions
Many expressions with *avoir* describe an emotion:

| | |
|---|---|
| *avoir confiance (en)* | to trust |
| *avoir peur (de)* | to be afraid |
| *avoir honte (de)* | to be ashamed of |
| *avoir de la peine* | to be sad |
| *avoir hâte (de)* | to be eager to, to be impatient to |

**"Félicitations!"**
You congratulate someone in French by saying *"Félicitations!"* or *"Je te félicite!"*

The verb *manquer* has a few meanings:

| | |
|---|---|
| *Tu me manques,* or *vous me manquez.* | I miss you. |
| *Il a manqué le train et son rendez-vous.* | He missed the train and his appointment. |
| *Elle a manqué son gateau.* | She ruined her cake. |

**False Cognate**
*Crier* means "to shout," NOT "to cry."

A great idiom (very colloquial) for expressing frustration is *J'en ai ras-le-bol!* which means roughly, "I've had it up to here!"

| | |
|---|---|
| *jurer* | to swear |
| *j'en ai marre / j'en ai assez* | I am fed up, I have had enough |
| *taquiner* | to tease |
| *se quereller* | to quarrel |
| *se disputer* | to have an argument / to argue |
| *se réconcilier avec* | to make up with |
| *se réjouir de* | to be delighted by |
| *prévoir* | to predict |
| *se souvenir de* | to remember |
| *soutenir* | to give support |
| *rompre (avec)* | to break up (with) |
| *se fâcher (avec)* | to get upset (at) |
| *se douter de quelque chose* | to suspect something |
| *sembler* | to seem |
| *craindre* | to fear, to be afraid of |

### It Seems to Me…

*Avoir l'air* means "to appear" or "to look."

*Elle a l'air fatigué.*

> She looks tired.

*Sentir* means "to smell" (having an odor or noticing an odor).

*Elle sent quelque chose de bon dans le four.*

> She can smell something nice in the oven.

*Ce poulet sent bon.*

> This chicken smells good.

*Se sentir* means "to feel."

*Comment te sens-tu aujourd'hui?*

> How do you feel today?

*Je me sens seul.*

> I feel lonely.

*Ressentir (+ noun)* means "to feel" (a pain or an emotion).

| | |
|---|---|
| *menacer* | to threaten |
| *avoir le coup de foudre pour* | to fall in love at first sight |
| *tomber amoureux de* | to fall in love (with) |
| *s'entendre* | to get along |
| *plaindre* | to feel sorry for |
| *en vouloir à* | to be angry at, to have a grudge against |
| *Ne t'en fais pas!* | Don't worry! |
| *Ça va s'arranger!* | It's going to get better! |
| *profiter de* | to take advantage of |
| *convaincre* | to convince |
| *ennuyeux / ennuyeuse* | boring |
| *ennuyé(e)* | bored, embarrassed, in trouble |
| *joyeux / joyeuse* | joyful |
| *heureux / heureuse* | happy |
| *content(e)* | glad, pleased, happy, content |
| *de bonne humeur* | in a good mood |
| *de mauvaise humeur* | in a bad mood |

| | |
|---|---|
| *triste* | sad |
| *fier / fière* | proud |
| *énervé(e)* | on edge, annoyed |
| *énervant(e)* | irritating |
| *comblé(e)* | fortunate, happy |
| *méchant(e)* | mean, nasty |
| *bassement* | meanly, nastily |
| *malheureux / malheureuse* | unhappy |
| *savant(e)* | learned, knowledgeable |
| *en colère, fâché(e)* | angry |
| *honteux / honteuse* | shameful, ashamed |
| *sage* | wise |
| *profond(e)* | profound or deep |
| *inquiet / inquiète* | worried |
| *préoccupé(e)* | worried |
| *déçu(e)* | disappointed |
| *tendu(e)* | uptight, tense |
| *ravi(e)* | delighted |
| *étonné(e)* | astonished |
| *ému(e)* | moved, touched |
| *fou / folle* | crazy |
| *dévoué(e) à* | devoted to |
| *exquis(e)* | exquisite |
| *bouleversé(e)* | overwhelmed |
| *vaniteux / vaniteuse* | vain |

## Les Expressions de Quantité

## Expressions of Quantity

| | |
|---|---|
| *le numéro* | number (as in digits) |
| *le nombre* | number (as in quantity) |
| *le compte* | count, account |
| *la somme* | sum |
| *les chiffres* | figures, numerals, digits |
| *évaluer* | to evaluate |
| *l'augmentation (f)* | increase / raise |
| *la croissance* | growth |

**Vocabulary**
If you want to tell someone to be happy, good, proud, etc., use the imperative of the verb *être* plus an adjective.
*Soyez sages!* Be good!
*Sois confiant!* Have faith! or Be confident!
*Sois fier!* Be proud!
*Sois content!* Be happy!

Work on your memorization: Regroup the verbs, nouns, and adjectives that carry the same meaning. Example: *la dévotion; se dévouer; dévoué.*

| | |
|---|---|
| *la subvention* | the subsidy |
| *le manque* | lack |
| *rien* | nothing |
| *tout* | everything |
| *tout le monde* | everybody |
| *beaucoup de* | a lot of, many |
| *un peu de* | a little of, a few |
| *peu de* | little / few |
| *trop de* | too many, too much |
| *moins de* | fewer, less than |
| *quelques* | some, a few |
| *aucun / aucune* | none, not any |
| *un tas de* | a stack of, many |
| *plein de* | full of |
| *le taux* | the rate |
| *les frais (m,pl.)* | expenses, costs |

The French school system is quite different from that of the U.S. By high school (*le lycée*), students have been divided into categories, each of which has a learning specialty: sciences, languages, economics, literature, etc. At the end of *le lycée*, students must pass a comprehensive exam in their specialty, *le baccalauréat (le bac)*, to graduate.

## L'école (f)          ## School

| | |
|---|---|
| *une bourse d'études* | a scholarship |
| *une sortie scolaire* | a field trip |
| *une moyenne* | a grade point average |
| *un carnet de notes* | a report card (elementary school) |
| *un bulletin scolaire* | a report card (secondary school) |
| *une interrogation* | a quiz, a test |
| *un dossier* | a file |
| *un débouché* | a career prospect |
| *une agrafeuse* | a stapler |
| *la colle* | glue |
| *un rapporteur* | a protractor |
| *un panneau d'affichage* | a bulletin board |
| *une bonne note* | a good grade |
| *une erreur* | a mistake |
| *feuilleter* | to leaf through |
| *permettre* | to permit, to allow |
| *traduire* | to translate |
| *écrire* | to write |

| | |
|---|---|
| *enseigner* | to teach |
| *parler couramment* | to speak fluently |
| *une dissertation* | an essay, a paper |
| *admettre* | to admit |
| *noter* | to grade |
| *suivre / prendre des cours* | to take classes |
| *souligner* | to underline |
| *faire une erreur / se tromper* | to make a mistake |
| *corriger* | to correct |
| *constater une erreur* | to notice a mistake |
| *passer un examen* | to take an exam |
| *rater* | to flunk / to fail |
| *sécher sur un sujet* | to draw a blank in |
| *sécher un cours* | to skip a class |
| *échouer à* | to fail |
| *être reçu(e) à un examen* | to pass an exam |
| *coller un(e) élève* | to give a detention to a student |
| *recaler* | to fail a student |
| *être recalé(e) à un examen* | to fail a test |
| *doué(e)* | gifted |
| *futé(e)* | smart |
| *perturbateur / perturbatrice* | disruptive |

**False Cognate**
*Passer un examen* means "to take an exam," NOT "to pass an exam."

## Les Sports (m)

## Sports

| | |
|---|---|
| *l'escrime* | fencing |
| *l'équitation* | horseback riding |
| *la natation* | swimming |
| *le parapente* | parasailing |
| *l'entraînement* | practice, training |
| *le vestiaire* | a locker room |
| *un but* | a goal |
| *la course* | a race |
| *le filet* | the net |
| *le cerceau* | the hoop |
| *une piste* | a trail, a track, a rink |
| *un terrain* | a ground, a field, a course |

| | |
|---|---|
| *un sifflet* | a whistle |
| *un arbitre* | a referee, an umpire |
| *une médaille* | a medal |
| *un exploit* | a feat |
| *le football* | soccer |
| *la Coupe du Monde* | the World Cup |
| *le poids* | weight |
| *tenter* | to attempt, to tempt |
| *atteindre* | to reach |
| *étendre le bras* | to stretch out one's arm |
| *entraîner* | to train, to coach |
| *s'entraîner* | to practice, to train |
| *attraper* | to catch |
| *lancer* | to throw |
| *accomplir* | to achieve |
| *sauter* | to jump |
| *s'assouplir* | to limber up, to become supple |
| *repousser* | to push back |
| *monter* | to go up |
| *escalader, grimper* | to climb |
| *être ex aequo / faire match nul* | to tie (as in scoring) |
| *souple* | flexible |
| *vif / vive* | quick, lively |
| *un coup déloyal(e)* | a foul |

| Les Faux Amis | | Common Mix-Ups | | |
|---|---|---|---|---|
| *la librairie* | bookstore | **and** | *la bibliothèque* | the library |
| *la gare* | the train station | **and** | *la station service* | the gas station |
| *le billet* | the ticket | **and** | *la facture* | the bill |
| *décevoir* | to disappoint | **and** | *tromper* | to deceive |
| *crier* | to shout, to scream | **and** | *pleurer* | to cry |
| *une course* | an errand | **and** | *un cours une classe* | a class, a course of study |
| *une course* | a race | **and** | *la race* | the race, the ethnicity |
| *le couvert* | the table setting, the cover charge | **and** | *la couverture* | the cover, the blanket |
| *blesser* | to wound, to hurt | **and** | *bénir* | to bless |
| *l'éditeur* | the publisher | **and** | *le rédacteur* | the editor |
| *le spectacle* | the show, the play | **and** | *les lunettes* | the eyeglasses |
| *l'agrément* | the pleasure, the approval | **and** | *l'accord* | the agreement |
| *le stage* | the training course, the internship | **and** | *la scène* | the stage |
| *la droguerie* | hardware store | **and** | *la pharmacie* | drugstore |
| *la location* | the rental | **and** | *le lieu/l'éndroit* | the location |
| *passer un examen* | to take an exam | **and** | *réussir un examen* | to pass an exam |

Only two or three questions on Part A will have tricky mix-ups.

**Vocabulary**
Vocabulary questions on Part C will often have mix-ups. Usually you will be given four words that are close in meaning or look alike.

| French words that look and sound similar but have different meanings | | | |
|---|---|---|---|
| *pleurer* | to cry | *pleuvoir* | to rain |
| *tromper* | to deceive | *tremper* | to soak |
| *vouloir* | to want | *en vouloir à* | to be angry at |
| *douter* | to doubt | *se douter de* | to suspect |

# Summary

Use the study techniques that work best for you and review the following categories of vocabulary:

- *Le calendrier et le temps*
- *Les expressions de temps*
- *La nature*
- *Le plein air*
- *La maison*
- *En ville*
- *Faire les courses*
- *Au restaurant*
- *Le monde du travail*
- *Le corps humain*
- *Les vêtements*
- *Les voyages / Les transports*
- *Les accidents et les urgences*
- *La maladie*
- *L'émotion*
- *Les expressions de quantité*
- *L'école*
- *Les sports*

# Chapter 5
# Grammar Review

Grammar is tested in Parts B and C of the SAT French Subject Test. Part B tests only grammar, while Part C tests both grammar and vocabulary. The same points of grammar are tested in Parts B and C. The SAT French Subject Test contains questions about very specific aspects of French grammar. Therefore, grammar is one of the easiest test topics on which to improve. If you can remember and master a few rules, you'll easily get more points. This chapter will explain exactly what you need to know. First, look at the point-by-point summary of the question types you can expect. Then, keep the question style in mind as you review your French grammar. Not all that you have learned in school will be included in the test, but you may find it helpful to go back to your textbooks for more examples on the topics we suggest. We focus on the grammatical topics and difficulties most often encountered on the SAT: pronouns, verbs, prepositions, and adverbs.

# PART B: GRAMMAR

Part B will consist of approximately 15 to 20 questions, arranged in order of difficulty. The first third of the questions will be considered easy, the next third will be of intermediate difficulty, and the final third will be the most challenging.

In these questions, there will be a sentence with a blank. You will choose the answer that is grammatically correct.

Become familiar with these directions that appear on the real test:

### Part B

**Directions:** Each of the following sentences contains a blank. From the four choices given, select the one that can be inserted in the blank to form a grammatically correct sentence and fill in the corresponding oval on the answer sheet. Choice (A) may consist of dashes that indicate that no insertion is required to form a grammatically correct sentence.

Jean-Claude est venu avec -------.

(A) ils
(B) leur
(C) eux
(D) soi

The correct answer is (C).

# PART C: COMPLETE THE PARAGRAPH

Part C tests both grammar and vocabulary. In this section, there are approximately 12 to 20 questions in no clear order of difficulty.

On this part of the test, several questions are combined in one paragraph. You may have three or four mini-paragraphs with three to five blanks within each, or you may have one long paragraph. You are asked to select the answers that best complete the sentences on the basis of either vocabulary or grammar.

Become familiar with these directions:

## Part C

**Directions:** The paragraphs below contain blank spaces indicating omissions in the text. For some blanks, it is necessary to choose the completion that is most appropriate to the meaning of the passage; for other blanks, you must choose the one completion that forms a grammatically correct sentence. In each case, indicate your answer by filling in the corresponding circle on the answer sheet. Be sure to read each paragraph completely before answering the questions related to it.

This section combines the characteristics of Parts A and B. The small differences between the two are discussed at the end of this chapter.

## KNOW WHAT YOU ARE LOOKING FOR

All the grammar questions on the SAT French Subject Test will fall into one of the following four categories.

1. pronouns
2. verbs
3. prepositions
4. odds and ends

The best way to improve in these areas is to learn the grammatical rules that are tested again and again. These rules are covered in the following grammar review.

## GRAMMAR REVIEW

Grammar is a great area to focus your attention for this test. Why? Because to do well on the grammar review you need to review only a limited number of rules. Those rules will lead you to the right answer again and again. Unlike vocabulary, where luck determines whether the words you've learned will show up, grammar rules—and therefore, the content of these test questions—stay the same.

You'll be tested primarily on three things: pronouns, verbs, and prepositions. Each question will address only one grammatical point. We'll cover each of these categories, giving you the rules that get you right answers. We'll also give practice

**Good News**
Only a minuscule number of grammar questions (around two) will test you on whether a noun is masculine or feminine.

questions for each category. Finally, we'll cover some odds and ends that occasionally show up on the test.

## BASIC TERMS

You won't be tested on this material directly, but take a quick look through to make sure that you understand what the following terms mean. We'll be using them in this grammar review.

## Parts of Speech

1. **Noun**—a person, place, thing, quality, or action. It can be either a subject or an object
2. **Verb**—the action that is being performed by the subject
3. **Pronoun**—a word that takes the place of a noun
4. **Preposition**—a word that expresses the relationship of one word to another in terms of direction, motion, or position
5. **Adjective**—a descriptive word that gives more information about a noun
6. **Adverb**—a word that modifies a verb, an adjective, or another adverb
7. **Article**—a small word that gives a little information about a noun

None of this terminology is needed for the test. Understanding these terms, however, will help you comprehend the explanations in the grammar review that follows.

## Sentence Structure

1. **Subject**—the person or thing in the sentence that is performing the action
2. **Compound subject**—two or more subjects joined by *and, or,* or *but*
3. **Object**—the person or thing that is on the receiving end of the action
4. **Direct object**—the word or phrase that receives the direct action of the verb. These do not take a preposition to be objects.
5. **Indirect object**—a word or phrase that precedes the direct object and answers the questions "to whom" or "for whom" the action of the verb is done. These take prepositions.
6. **Infinitive**—the form of a verb that uses "to," as in "to go" or "to speak"
7. **Auxiliary verb**—a helper verb, either *avoir* or *être,* that loses its own meaning to help form the compound past tense for other verbs, such as the *passé composé.* It is followed by the past participle of the conjugated verb.

8. **Semi-auxiliary verb**—a verb, such as *aller* or *venir*, that helps express a different aspect of the verbal action, such as the near future or the recent past

9. **Past participle**—in the past tense, the form of the verb that teams up with the auxiliary or "helper" verb

| Mom and Dad | gave | me | a car | for graduation. |
|---|---|---|---|---|
| compound subject | verb | indirect object | direct object | prepositional phrase |
| **They** | **baked** | **a** | **delicious** | **cake.** |
| subject pronoun | verb | article | adjective | direct object |

# PRONOUNS

A quarter of all grammar questions on the SAT French test will challenge your knowledge of pronouns. Unlike English, which uses mainly subject and object forms of pronouns (he and him, for example), French uses four important forms of pronouns: subject pronouns, direct object pronouns, indirect object pronouns, and stressed pronouns.

## What Is a Pronoun?

A pronoun takes the place of a noun. It stands in for the full name or description of a person, place, or thing. In French, a pronoun will take different forms depending on what type of noun it replaces. Half of the pronoun questions on the test ask you to choose among subject pronouns, direct or indirect object pronouns, and stressed pronouns.

The following are the pronouns you should know. **You're most likely to be tested on third-person singular and plural,** since these are the forms that change the most.

| Subjects | Objects | | Reflexive | Stressed |
|---|---|---|---|---|
| | **Direct** | **Indirect** | | |
| *je* | *me (m')* | *me (m')* | *me (m')* | *moi* |
| *tu* | *te (t')* | *te (t')* | *te (t')* | *toi* |
| *il, elle* | *le, la (l')* | *lui* | *se, (s')* | *lui, elle* |
| *nous* | *nous* | *nous* | *nous* | *nous* |
| *vous* | *vous* | *vous* | *vous* | *vous* |
| *ils, elles* | *les* | *leur* | *se (s')* | *eux, elles* |

Once you recognize each of these four main types of pronouns, you will find it easy to use Process of Elimination on the answer choices.

Because this is a multiple-choice test, you will be asked which of four pronouns goes into the blank. Notice that some pronouns are always the same: *nous* and *vous*.

| | |
|---|---|
| *nous* or *vous* can be: | subject |
| | direct object |
| | indirect object |
| | reflexive |
| | stressed |

**Vocabulary**
The subject pronouns *il, ils, elle,* and *elles* are used for objects and people. *Il* signifies "he" or "it." *Elle* signifies "she" or "it." The subject pronoun *il* can be neutral or impersonal: *il est sept heures, il pleut, il faut que…* The subject pronoun *ils* is used for a group of males and for mixed groups, even if there are more females than males.

# 1. Subject Pronouns

Subject pronouns replace the subject of the sentence.

*Jean a montré son dessin à Edith.*
> **Jean** showed his drawing to Edith.

*Il a montré son dessin à Edith.*
> **He** showed his drawing to Edith.

| | | | | | |
|---|---|---|---|---|---|
| *je* or *j'* | = | I | *nous* | = | we |
| *tu* | = | you | *vous* | = | you (plural or formal singular) |
| *il* | = | he | *ils* | = | they (masculine) |
| *elle* | = | she | *elles* | = | they (feminine) |

These pronouns are usually the wrong answer choices. Why? Because these are the pronouns with which everyone is most familiar and comfortable.

# 2. Direct Object Pronouns

These pronouns replace the direct object of a sentence. The direct object answers the question "what?"

*Jean a montré **son dessin** à Edith.*
> Jean showed **his drawing** to Edith.

*Jean **l'a** montré à Edith.*
> Jean showed **it** (the drawing) to Edith.

Notice that the direct object pronoun is placed before the verb.

| | | | | | |
|---|---|---|---|---|---|
| *me* or *m'* | = | me | *nous* | = | us |
| *te* or *t'* | = | you | *vous* | = | you (plural or formal) |
| *le* or *l'* | = | him or it | *les* | = | them (person or thing both masculine and feminine) |
| *la* or *l'* | = | her or it | | | |

**Pronouns**

When a direct object pronoun comes before a verb that starts with a vowel, the vowel in the pronoun is dropped and replaced with an apostrophe. For example, *me* becomes *m´* and *le* or *la* becomes *l´*.

## 3. Indirect Object Pronouns

These pronouns replace the indirect object of a sentence. The indirect object answers the questions "to what?" or "to whom?" Notice that the pronoun replaces both the indirect object and the preposition that goes with it.

> *Jean a montré son dessin à Edith.*
> Jean showed his drawing **to Edith**.

> *Jean **lui** a montré son dessin.*
> Jean showed **her** his drawing.

| | | | | | |
|---|---|---|---|---|---|
| *me* or *m'* | = | me | *nous* | = | us |
| *te* or *t'* | = | you | *vous* | = | you (plural or formal) |
| *lui* | = | him or her | *leur* | = | them |

**Pronouns**

Notice that the indirect object pronoun is placed before the verb.

Review the list of verbs that take the prepositions *de* or *à* (or both), and their meaning. Some of them are listed on page 105 of this book.

Pay particular attention to the following verbs:

The verbs *écouter* (to listen to), *regarder* (to look at), and *attendre* (to wait for) are verbs that always take a **direct object** in French.

> *Il m'écoute.*
> He listens (to) me.

> *Je l'ai regardez.*
> I looked (at) him.

> *Nous les attendons.*
> We are waiting (for) them.

**Pronouns**

Note that the only differences between direct and indirect object pronouns occur in the third person singular and plural forms: *le/la/l'* vs. *lui* and *les* vs. *leur*. You are more likely to be tested on these, as you have to know the rules in order to figure out which pronoun is correct.

The verbs *téléphoner à* (to call on the phone), *répondre à* (to answer), *demander à* (to ask), and *rendre visite à* (to visit someone), take an **indirect object** in French, unlike in English.

> *Ton père te téléphone.*
>> Your father is calling you.

> *Je résponds à la question du professeur.*
>> I answer the teacher's question.

> *Sa mère lui demande de nettoyer sa chambre.*
>> Her mother is asking her to clean her room.

> *Cette semaine, il rends visite à son grandpère.*
>> He is visiting his grandfather this week.

The direct and indirect object pronouns are placed before the verb even when you use the negative form.

> *Je ne te donne pas mon nouveau pull.*
>> I will not give you my new sweater.

> *Il ne leur parle pas.*
>> He does not speak to them.

## 4. Reflexive Pronouns

The reflexive pronoun shows that the action is being performed both by and to the subject. Only certain verbs have reflexive forms. Most often reflexives will show up as incorrect answer choices.

**Pronouns**

Reflexive pronouns are used in French in situations in which they are not used in English. For example, *Je me lave les mains* (I wash my hands).

*Tu te laves.*
　　You wash yourself.

*Tu te laves les mains.*
　　You wash your hands.

| | | | |
|---|---|---|---|
| *me* | myself | *nous* | ourselves |
| *te* | yourself | *vous* | yourselves or yourself (formal) |
| *se* | himself/herself | *se* | themselves |

You might also see *moi-même, toi-même, lui-même/elle-même, soi-même* (oneself), *nous-mêmes, vous-même(s), eux-mêmes / elles-mêmes*. They would be used as stressed pronouns would be.

> *Tu te coupes **toi-même** les cheveux!*
>> You cut your hair **yourself**!

All reflexive verbs take the auxiliary *être* in the compound tenses. If the verb has no object, the past participle always agrees with the subject:

> *Elles se sont dépêchées.*          They hurried.
> *Elle s'est coupée.*          She cut herself.

However, there is no agreement in the sentence when the body part, or direct object, comes after the reflexive verb. We'll talk more about this later in the review.

> *Elles se sont lavé les mains.*          They washed their hands.

## Pronoun Order

If the sentence contains both a direct and an indirect pronoun, order the pronouns as shown in the chart below.

| Indirect Object | before | Direct Object | before | Indirect Object |
|---|---|---|---|---|
| *me* | | *le* | | *lui* |
| *te* | | *la* | | |
| *nous* | before | *l'* | before | |
| *vous* | | *les* | | *leur* |

> *Tu donnes le cadeau à ta sœur. Tu **le lui** donnes maintenant.*
>> You give the present to your sister. You give **it to her** now.

> *Tu écris cette lettre à ton frère. Oui, je **la lui** écris.*
>> You write a letter to your brother. Yes, I write **it to him**.

> *Je vous prête mes livres. Je **vous les** prête.*
>> I lend my books to you. I lend **them to you**.

## Pronoun Order with Commands

In negative commands, the order of pronouns follows the same rule:

> *Ne **le lui** rends pas!*
>> Don't give **it** back **to him!**

> *Ne **me les** donne pas!*
>> Don't give **them to me!**

In affirmative commands, the *me* becomes *moi*, and the direct or indirect pronoun (*moi, nous…*) is placed after the verb.

> *Appelle-**moi** ce soir!*
>> Call **me** tonight.

> *Répondez-**nous** tout de suite.*
>> Give **us** an answer right away.

When the command contains a direct pronoun and an indirect pronoun, both pronouns come after the verb. Follow the order below:

| Direct Object | before | Indirect Object |
|---|---|---|
| *le* | | *moi* |
| *la* | before | *lui* |
| *les* | | *nous* |
| | | *leur* |

> *Donne-**les-moi**!*
>> Give them to me!

> *Rends-**le-lui**!*
>> Give it back to her!

## Pronouns *y* and *en*

These are adverbial pronouns. Remember that *y* comes before *en,* and that indirect objects always precede both.

> *Il **y** a beaucoup de fraises au marché ce matin. Il **y en** a beaucoup.*
>> **There** are lots of strawberries at the market this morning. **There** are lots **of them.**

> *Il rend visite à sa tante à l'hôpital. Il **lui y** rend visite tous les jours.*
>> He visits his aunt at the hospital. He visits **her there** every day.

*Nous rencontrons souvent nos amis au cinéma. Nous **les y** rencontrons souvent*

> We often meet our friends at the movies. We meet **them there** often.

*Tu **m'y** retrouves à six heures.*

> You meet **me there** at six o'clock.

These pronouns are often seen in negative and affirmative commands:

*Achète-**lui-en**!*
> Buy **him/her some**!

*Ne **leur en** prête pas!*
> Don't lend **them any**!

*Occupe-**t'en** tout de suite!*
> [**You**] Take care **of it** right away!

## 5. Stressed Pronouns

Stressed pronouns are used only to replace nouns representing people or animals.

| | | | | | |
|---|---|---|---|---|---|
| ***moi*** | = | me or I | ***nous*** | = | us or we |
| ***toi*** | = | you | ***vous*** | = | you (plural or formal) |
| ***lui*** | = | him or he | ***eux*** | = | them or they (masculine or including both masculine and feminine) |
| ***elle*** | = | her or she | ***elles*** | = | them or they (feminine) |

### Uses of the Stressed Pronoun

#### A. After a preposition such as *à, pour, avec, sans, chez* …

*Elle pense à sa sœur. Elle pense à **elle**.*
> She thinks of **her sister**. She thinks of **her**.

*Je travaille pour **mes patrons**. Je travaille pour **eux**.*
> I work for **my bosses**. I work for **them**.

*Je vis avec **mon père**. Je vis avec **lui**.*
> I live with **my father**. I live with **him**.

*Tu vas au cinéma sans **ton frère**. Tu vas au cinéma sans **lui**.*
> You go to the movies without **your brother**. You go to the movies without **him**.

*Tu peux rester chez **mes tantes**. Tu peux rester chez **elles**.*
You can stay at **my aunts'** house. You can stay at **their** house.

## B. To reinforce a subject pronoun. There is no real English equivalent.

***Moi**, je parle très bien le français.*
[Myself], I speak French very well.

***Vous**, vous êtes parfait!*
[Yourself], You are perfect!

## C. After the expressions *c'est* and *ce n'est pas* and, of course, their various conjugated forms.

*C'est **ton frère** qui est avec cette fille? Non, ce n'est pas **lui**.*
Is it **your brother** who is with this girl? No, it is not (**he**).

## D. Before and after *et* and *ou*.

***Toi** et **lui**, vous allez bien vous amuser.*
**You** and **he** are going to have fun.

## E. In short sentences with no verb.

*Qui a demandé un chocolat? C'est **moi**.*
Who asked for a chocolate? **Me**. (I did.)

# 6. Demonstrative Pronouns

The demonstrative pronoun *celui* (this / the one) is used instead of *ce* + noun or *le* + noun.

It agrees in gender and number with the noun it replaces: *celui, celle, ceux, celles*.

There are a few combinations to keep in mind:

a.  In a composed form
    *celui-ci, celui-là, ceux-ci, celles-ci, celle-là...*
    *Voilà les robes blanches. Ce sont **celles**-ci que j'aime.*
    Here are the white dresses. **These** are the ones I like.

b.  With the preposition *de*
    *Ce ne sont pas mes sandales. Ce sont **celles** de Sophie.*
    These are not my sandals. **These** are Sophie's.

c.  With *qui, que,* or *dont*. (See the use of these pronouns in the next section.)
    *J'aime les robes blanches, surtout **celles** qui sont à la mode.*
    I like white dresses, especially the trendy **ones**.

**Keep These In Mind**

d.  *Ce* is the neutral simple form and is used with the verb *être*.
    *C'est toujours bon de se revoir!*
    **It's** always nice to see each other again.

e.  *Ceci* and *cela* are the compound neutral forms.
    *Cela me donne une idée.*
    **This** gives me an idea.

# 7. Interrogative Pronouns

The interrogative pronoun *lequel* (which one) is used sometimes to replace *quel* + noun.

> *Quel livre préfères-tu?*
> **Which book** do you prefer?

> *Lequel préfères-tu?*
> **Which one** do you prefer?

It agrees in gender and number with the noun it replaces: *lequel, laquelle, lesquels, lesquelles.*

See the table below for the use of these pronouns with prepositions *à* and *de*:

| of (which one) | about (which one) |
|---|---|
| *à + laquelle = à laquelle* | *de + laquelle = de laquelle* |
| *à + lequel = auquel* | *de + lequel = duquel* |
| *à + lesquels = auxquels* | *de + lesquels = desquels* |
| *à + lesquelles = auxquelles* | *de + lesquelles = desquelles* |

> *J'ai deux frères. **Duquel** me parles-tu? (= de quel frère?)*
> I have two brothers. **Which one** are you talking about?

> *Il y a plusieurs classes à choisir pour ce niveau. **Auxquelles** voulez-vous participer? (= à quelles classes?)*
> There are several classes to choose from at this level. **Which ones** do you want to attend?

Let's practice our pronoun skills.

---

Paul voulait ------- faire peur.

(A) elle
(B) la
(C) lui
(D) les

## Here's How to Crack It

Does the missing pronoun here serve as a subject or object? It serves as an object, so we can eliminate (A). *Elle* serves only as a subject pronoun or a stressed pronoun. We won't use a stressed pronoun because a preposition is not being used.

Does the verb *faire peur* take a direct or indirect object? Indirect. In English, "to frighten someone" takes a direct object, but in French the expression is *faire peur à quelqu'un.*

Often, three choices will refer to one person, the fourth to more than one person. In most cases, the one that is different will be wrong.

Let's cross out (D) *les,* which is a direct object pronoun as well as the only plural pronoun.

So, which choice is an indirect object pronoun?

*Lui,* (C), is the indirect pronoun for third person singular. It is the right answer. *La,* (B), is the direct object pronoun.

---

Je suis allé au concert sans -------.

(A) leur
(B) tu
(C) le
(D) eux

What type of pronoun would come after *sans*? A stressed pronoun comes after a preposition. Which of the answer choices is a stressed pronoun? Only (D). *Eux* is the stressed pronoun meaning "them." (A) is an indirect object pronoun. (B) is a subject pronoun. (C) is a direct object pronoun. (D) is the correct answer: *Je suis allé au concert sans eux.*

## More Types of Pronouns

You also want to be familiar with some other types of pronouns that may show up. The following are most likely to appear on the real test as incorrect answer choices.

### Possessive Pronouns

Possessive pronouns agree in gender and number with the noun that they replace.

| | |
|---|---|
| *Ce livre est à Nathalie.* | *C'est le sien.* |
| This book is Nathalie's. | It is hers. |
| | (use of possessive pronoun) |
| *Cette montre est à Pierre.* | *C'est la sienne.* |
| This watch is Pierre's. | It is his. |

### Singular Pronouns

| | |
|---|---|
| *le mien / la mienne* | *le nôtre / la nôtre* |
| *le tien / la tienne* | *le vôtre / la vôtre* |
| *le sien / la sienne* | *le leur / la leur* |
| | |
| *Ce livre est à toi.* | *C'est le tien.* |
| This book is yours. | It is yours. |

### Plural pronouns

| | |
|---|---|
| *les miens / les miennes* | *les nôtres* |
| *les tiens / les tiennes* | *les vôtres* |
| *les siens / les siennes* | *les leurs* |
| | |
| *Ces chaussures sont à elles.* | *Ce sont les leurs.* |
| These shoes are theirs. | They are theirs. |

Possessive pronouns must always be used with an article (*le, la, les*).

| Person | Singular | | Plural | |
|---|---|---|---|---|
| | **Masculine** | **Feminine** | **Masculine** | **Feminine** |
| *je* | *le mien* | *la mienne* | *les miens* | *les miennes* |
| *tu* | *le tien* | *la tienne* | *les tiens* | *les tiennes* |
| *il, elle* | *le sien* | *la sienne* | *les siens* | *les siennes* |
| *nous* | *le nôtre* | *la nôtre* | *les nôtres** | |
| *vous* | *le vôtre* | *la vôtre* | *les vôtres** | |
| *ils, elles* | *le leur* | *la leur* | *les leurs** | |

*These represent both the masculine and the feminine forms.

## Still More Types of Pronouns

About half of the pronoun questions revolve around the use of other types of pronouns (adverbial pronouns, demonstrative pronouns, relative pronouns, indefinite pronouns, etc.). Don't worry—you don't need to know the terminology.

Example:

> Je n'ai pas le temps de faire les courses ------- ma mère m'a demandé de faire.
>
> (A) qui
> (B) que
> (C) dont
> (D) lesquelles

Which pronoun is correct?

Let's take a look at each in turn and see what rules govern their use.

## *Qui*—Who or Which or That

**Qui** vs. **Que**
Don't use your ear to determine if **qui** or **que** is right. Learn a few rules that will help you choose: 1. Is the noun before the blank the subject or object of the phrase? 2. Is there a preposition involved?

*Qui* is the equivalent of the English "who," except that *qui* can also be used to refer to things ("that"). **The *qui* refers to the subject of the phrase.**

> *la dame **qui** danse là-bas . . .*
> the lady **who** is dancing over there . . .

> *la table **qui** est cassée . . .*
> the table **that** is broken . . .

*Qui* can also be used with a preposition. In this case, it can only refer to a person.

> *l'homme sans **qui** je n'aurais rien accompli . . .*
> the man without **whom** I would have accomplished nothing . . .

## Ce qui—What

*Ce qui* is used as the subject of the sentence or clause.

> *Qu'est-ce qui se passe?*
>> **What** is happening?

> *Je ne sais pas ce qui la fait pleurer!*
>> I do not know **what**'s making her cry!

## Que—Whom or That

*Que* is used in a number of ways in the French language. On the SAT French Test, however, it usually shows up as a relative pronoun. Roughly the equivalent of the English "whom," it refers to the person or thing that is **the object** of the action. **Que is never used with a preposition.**

> *l'enfant que j'ai puni . . .*
> (i.e., *j'ai puni l'enfant*)
>> the child **whom** I punished . . .

> *la bicyclette que j'ai reçue pour mon anniversaire . . .*
> (i.e., *j'ai reçu la bicyclette pour mon anniversaire*)
>> the bicycle **that** I received for my birthday . . .

## Ce que—What

*Ce que* is used as a direct object in a sentence or clause.

> *Je ne comprends pas ce qu'il dit.*
>> I do not understand **what** he is saying.

> *Je préfère ce que tu viens d'acheter.*
>> I prefer **what** you have just bought.

## When Do You Use *Qui* and When Do You Use *Que*?

Unless there is a preposition involved, this is similar to the English use of "who" or "whom." In English, one test is to see if the "who" or "whom" would be replaced by "he" or "him."

> the man _____ is smoking over there . . .
>> "He" is smoking, so you would use "who."

> the man _____ I hugged . . .
>> I hugged "him," so you would use "whom."

If you understand "who/whom" in English, you may want to translate and decide if "who" or "whom" is correct. If "who" is correct, use *qui;* if "whom" is correct, use *que.*

> *l'homme qui fume là-bas . . .*
> the man **who** is smoking over there . . .

> *l'homme que j'ai embrassé . . .*
> the man **whom** I hugged . . .

## What If a Preposition Is Involved?

If a preposition is involved and the pronoun refers to a person, use *qui* or the correct form of *lequel.*

> *l'homme à qui j'ai donné de l'argent . . .*
> the man **to whom** I gave money . . .

> *l'ami pour lequel j'ai acheté un chapeau . . .*
> the friend **for whom** I bought a hat . . .

> *la jeune fille pour laquelle j'ai fait une robe . . .*
> the girl **for whom** I made a dress . . .

*Lequel* is used with a preposition if the pronoun refers to people or things. The form of *lequel* agrees in gender and number with the person(s) or thing(s) it refers to.

Note that if a preposition is involved and the pronoun refers to a thing, use only *lequel* (in its correct form).

> *l'argent avec lequel j'ai payé la facture . . .*
> the money **with which** I paid the bill . . .

## *Quoi*—Which or What

*Quoi* is used to refer to things only. It is usually used with a preposition when asking a question.

> *À quoi pensez-vous?*
> **What** are you thinking of?

> *De quoi parlez-vous?*
> **What** are you talking about?

*De quoi* is also used in many idiomatic expressions, such as:

> *avoir de quoi faire*
> to have a lot to do

---

*If there is a preposition before the blank, you use qui if referring to a person, and the correct form of lequel if referring to a thing or a person. You never use que immediately following a preposition.*

*Lequel, laquelle, lesquels, and lesquelles, are always used after the prepositions entre, sans, parmi, and avant.*

*avoir de quoi manger*
> to have something to eat

*avoir de quoi vivre*
> to have enough to live on

*Merci beaucoup! Il n'y a pas de quoi!*
> Many thanks! Don't mention it!

## Ce à quoi—What

*Ce à quoi* is used to emphasize an idea, but it is mostly avoided otherwise.

*Ce à quoi il faut toujours faire attention, c'est l'utilisation des pronoms.*
> **What** you must always pay attention to is the use of pronouns.

## Avec quoi—With What

*Je voudrais savoir avec quoi il a fait cela.*
> I would like to know **with what** he did this.

## Sans quoi—Otherwise, If Not

*Si tu fais tes devoirs tu pourras sortir; sans quoi tu resteras ici.*
> If you do your homework, you can go out; **otherwise**, you'll stay here.

## Dont—Of Whom or Of Which

*Dont* is correct only if the verb in the phrase is one that takes *de* as a preposition. *Dont* is always placed directly after the noun it replaces.

*Le livre dont j'ai besoin est dans ma chambre.*
> The book **that** I need is in my room.

*L'ami dont elle a parlé viendra chez nous ce soir.*
> The friend **of whom** she spoke will come to our house this evening.

When it is separated by a preposition, use *duquel, de laquelle, desquels, desquelles.*

*L'homme à côté duquel le chien attend nous a salués.*
> The man next to **whom** the dog waits greeted us.

*Les gens à côté desquels nous étions assis n'ont pas arrêté de parler.*
> The people next to **whom** we were sitting did not stop talking.

## *Ce dont*—What

*Ce dont* is used as an object with a verb that takes the preposition *de*.

> *Il ne comprend pas ce dont j'ai besoin.*
>> He does not understand **what** I need.

> *J'ai oublié ce dont elle m'a parlé.*
>> I forgot **what** she talked to me about.

Now let's go back to our example first given on page 76.

---

Je n'ai pas le temps de faire les courses ------- ma mère m'a demandé de faire.

(A) qui
(B) que
(C) dont
(D) lesquelles

### Here's How to Crack It

Is a preposition involved? No. Get rid of (D) *lesquelles*. You can also get rid of (A) *qui*, because where objects are concerned, *qui* is used only with a preposition.

Does *faire* take *de* as a preposition? No. Eliminate (C) *dont*. The answer must be (B) *que*.

---

Voilà l'ami ------- j'ai passé l'été.

(A) chez qui
(B) à qui
(C) que
(D) dont

### Here's How to Crack It

Can *de* be used as a preposition following *passer l'été*? No. Eliminate (D).

Can *passer l'été* be used without a preposition? No. Eliminate (C) *que*.

You can use *à* with *passer l'été*, but in that case it would be used with a place, not with a person. Eliminate (B).

Can *passer l'été* be used with *chez*? Yes. *Passer l'été chez* means "to spend the summer at the home of." (A) is the right answer.

———————⌒———————

## *Où*—Where

*Voilà la bibliothèque où j'ai passé beaucoup de temps.*
> There is the library **where** I spent a lot of time.

*J'ai vu l'hôpital où je suis né.*
> I saw the hospital **where** I was born.

*Où* can in many cases be replaced by *dans lequel* (*laquelle/lesquels/lesquelles*).

*Où* means **when** after the expressions *au moment, à l'époque, au temps,* and *le jour.* Use this carefully and only when it could be replaced by *pendant lequel.*

*Les jours où il n'y avait plus de pain, ils mangeaient du riz.*
> On the days **when** there was no more bread, they ate rice.

*Où* and *dans lequel* sometimes mean the same thing. You'll never be asked to choose between the two.

## *En*—Of It/Of Them

*En* replaces a noun that is used with a verb that takes the preposition *de*. It can be used for people or things. It is often used in sentences that refer to a number or quantity of things.

*Nous parlons du livre.*
> We are speaking about the book.

*Nous en parlons.*
> We are speaking **about** it.

Think of *en* as meaning "of it" or "of them." You can use it in some cases where the *de* is understood but not actually used.

*J'ai des cassettes.*
> I have some tapes.

*J'ai cinq cassettes.*
> I have five tapes.

*J'en ai cinq.*
> I have five **of them.**

While *en* will usually refer to some kind of possession, it can also be used to indicate place or location if the verb in question uses *de*.

> *Il vient de Rome.*
> > He comes from Rome.

> *Il en vient.*
> > He's coming **from there**.

## *Y*—There

*Y* often refers to place or location. *Y* replaces phrases that begin with prepositions that indicate place (*à, chez, dans, sur*).

> *Est-ce que tu vas à la fête?*
> > Are you going to the party?

> *Oui, j'y vais.*
> > Yes, I am going **there**.

*Y*, an indirect object pronoun, also replaces a thing or an idea that is preceded by the preposition *à*.

> *Tu crois au Père Noël?*
> > You believe in Santa?

> *Oui, j'y crois!*
> > Yes, I do!

> *Jouez-vous au tennis?*
> > Do you play tennis?

> *Oui, j'y joue.*
> > Yes, I do.

> *As-tu réfléchi à ta dissertation?*
> > Have you thought about your essay?

> *Oui, j'y ai réfléchi.*
> > Yes, I have.

## *Chacun*—Each One

> *Chacun à son tour!*
> > Wait your turn!

> *On a trois euros chacun.*
> > We each have three euros.

## Quelques-uns/unes (de)—Some (Of)

*Quelques-uns de ces livres sont à lire avant la fin du semestre.*
> **Some of** those books are to be read before the end of the semester.

*Je peux goûter ces bonbons?*
> May I taste these candies?

*Oui, prends en **quelques-uns.***
> Yes, take **some of** them.

## Aucun/Aucune—Not One, None

*Je n'en aime **aucun!***
> I like **none** of them!

*Aucun* and *aucune* are always used with *ne*.

*Aucune de ces réponses n'est correcte.*
> **None** of these answers is correct.

## Quelqu'un—Someone

*Quelqu'un a volé ma moto!*
> **Someone** stole my motorcycle!

## Personne—No One

*Est-ce que quelqu'un a vu le voleur?*
> Did anyone see the thief?

*Non, **personne** ne l'a vu.*
> No, **no one** saw him.

Like *aucun*, *personne* is used with *ne*. *Personne* can be used without the *ne* only if it is a one-word answer to a question.

*Qui a cassé ce vase?*
> Who broke this vase?

*Personne.*
> No one.

## Quelque chose—Something

*Je vous ai acheté **quelque chose** à la pâtisserie.*
> I bought you **something** at the pastry shop.

Both *aucun* and *personne* must be used with *ne* in a sentence.

### *Ne…rien*—Nothing

*Est-ce que tu as acheté quelque chose à la pâtisserie?*
> Did you buy something at the pastry shop?

*Non, je n'ai rien acheté.*
> No, I did **not** buy **anything**.

---

Avez-vous des stylos? -------.

(A) Oui, lesquels.
(B) Oui, j'ai quelques.
(C) Non, je n'en ai aucun.
(D) Non, je n'ai pas.

### Here's How to Crack It

(A) *lesquels* cannot stand by itself in a sentence unless it is an answer to a question (*Apporte-moi les stylos. Lesquels?*). Eliminate it.

(B) *quelques*, meaning "some," is an adjective and can only be used to modify a noun (*j'ai quelques stylos* or *j'en ai quelques-uns*). Eliminate it.

(C) *aucun* is used with *ne*. This is correct.

(D) By itself, *je n'ai pas* does not work. It lacks a reference to what it is that I do not have. To be correct, you would need to say either *je n'en ai pas* or *je n'ai pas de stylos*.

---
---

Qui va chercher le paquet à la poste? ------- vais.

(A) A quoi
(B) J'y
(C) Personne
(D) J'en

### Here's How to Crack It

(A), *A quoi* does not work and makes no sense. It refers to things and is usually used with a preposition.

(B) is correct. The *y* replaces the expression *à la poste*.

(C) has two problems. First, *personne* needs to be used with *ne*. Second, *personne* takes the third person singular form of the verb (in this case, *va*).

(D) *En* is used to show either possession or to replace a noun that works with a verb that takes *de*. Here the verb is *aller* and it takes the preposition *à*. So *en* is not correct.

———————————◯———————————

# DRILL 1: PRONOUN QUESTIONS
Answers can be found in Part III.

1. ------- est arrivé à Paul hier?

   (A) Quel
   (B) Quoi
   (C) Qu'
   (D) Qu'est-ce qui

2. C'est -------.

   (A) eux
   (B) il
   (C) lui
   (D) le

3. C'est grâce à ------- que nous avons pu venir.

   (A) eux
   (B) les
   (C) leur
   (D) ils

4. La chose la plus difficile est de ------- réveiller le matin.

   (A) lui
   (B) il
   (C) le
   (D) moi

5. ------- a sorti la poubelle.

   (A) Il n'
   (B) Personne n'
   (C) Aucun
   (D) Qui

# VERBS

There are three areas that verb questions tend to test: use of the subjunctive, agreement of the past participle, and tense.

## Know the Subjunctive

About 25 percent of the grammar questions on the test deal with verb use. Over half of them ask you to decide whether or not to use the subjunctive.

## What Is the Subjunctive?

Like the indicative, the subjunctive is not a tense; it is a mode or mood. While it is not often used in English, it is used very frequently in French. This is why it is always found on the SAT French Subject Test.

You must use the indicative mode with verbs expressing an opinion, such as *penser que, croire que, espérer que, être sûr que, être certain que* when they are used in the affirmative form.

> *Je crois que vous avez raison.*
> I believe you are right.

> *Nous pensons que tes parents seront contents de te revoir.*
> We think your parents will be happy to see you again.

> *J'espère que vous allez bien.*
> I hope you are well.

Compare the above examples to the following examples, which display these verbs used in the negative form. The negative form makes a difference!

> *Je ne crois pas qu'il ait raison.*
> I don't think he's right.

> *Nous ne pensons pas que tes parents soient contents.*
> We don't think your parents are happy.

## When Do You Use the Subjunctive?

In French and on the SAT French, you will use the subjunctive in phrases that follow expressions of doubt, suggestion, preference, desire, improbability, or emotion. The subjunctive is also used with certain conjunctions. All phrases that require use of the subjunctive will contain the word *que*.

## Expressions That Take the Subjunctive

### Doubt or Uncertainty

*Je doute qu'il réussisse son examen.*
I doubt that he will pass his exam.

*J'ai peur qu'il rate son examen.*
I am afraid that he will fail his exam.

*Je ne crois pas que vous ayez raison.*
I don't believe that you are right.

*Il est douteux qu'elle vienne ce weekend.*
It's doubtful that she will come this weekend.

*Il est possible que j'aie tort.*
I may be wrong. (It is possible that I am wrong.)

## Suggestion or Preference

*Je préfère que vous rentriez tout de suite.*

  I **prefer that** you return at once.

*Je tiens à ce que tu sois à l'heure.*

  I **insist that** you be on time.

*Il vaut mieux que vous ne sortiez pas ce soir.*

  It is **better that** you do not go out tonight.

*Il est important que vous étudiez l'emploi du subjonctif.*

  It is **important that** you study the use of the subjunctive.

*Il faut que je prenne un rendez-vous chez le dentiste.*

  It is **necessary that** I make an appointment at the dentist's.

## Desire

*Je veux que tu travailles plus sérieusement.*

  I **want** you to work more seriously.

*Je souhaite que tout se passe bien.*

  I **wish that** everything goes well.

*Je désire qu'il soit heureux.*

  I **want** him to be happy.

## Improbability

*Il est peu probable qu'il neige demain.*

  It is **unlikely that** it will snow tomorrow.

Note: **Do not use the subjunctive with probability.**

*Il est probable qu'il pleuvra demain.*

  It is likely that it will rain tomorrow.

## Emotion

*Je suis étonné qu'il ne soit pas encore là.*

  I **am surprised** that he is not yet here.

*Je suis content que tout se soit bien passé.*

  I **am happy that** everything went well.

*Je regrette que le temps passe si vite.*

  I **am sorry that** time goes by so quickly.

All phrases that require use of the subjunctive will contain the word *que.*

The subjunctive is used with expressions of doubt, preference, or emotion.

## Superlative

*Cet homme est le seul qui sache encore travailler de ses mains.*
> **This man is the only one who** still knows how to work with his hands.

*C'est la meilleure nouvelle que vous puissiez lui donner.*
> **It is the best news that** you can give him.

## Expressions That DO NOT Take the Subjunctive

**Pay Attention to Improbabilities**
It is unlikely to be beautiful tomorrow.

The following expressions do not take the subjunctive when they are used in the affirmative form only:

| | |
|---|---|
| *il est probable que* | it is likely |
| *espérer* | to hope |
| *se demander* | to wonder |
| *croire* | to believe |
| *penser* | to think |
| *se douter que* | to suspect |

*Il est probable qu'il neigera demain.*
> It is probably going to snow tomorrow.

*Je me demande s'il viendra.*
> I wonder if he will come.

Beware of *ne* used as an expletive after *avant que, de peur que, de crainte que, avoir peur que, craindre que,* and *à moins que.* It is not a negative form, but only substantiates an already-negative main clause, such as in expressions of fear, warning, or doubt.

*Je vais aller me promener avant qu'il ne pleuve.*
> I will go for a walk before it rains.

*Je crains qu'il ne pleuve.*
> I am afraid it might rain.

## Conjunctions That Take the Subjunctive

| | |
|---|---|
| *pour que, de manière (à ce) que* | so that |
| *de sorte que, afin que* | so that |
| *quoique, bien que* | although |
| *pourvu que, à condition que* | provided that, so long as |
| *à moins que* | unless |
| *jusqu'à ce que* | until |
| *en attendant que* | waiting for |
| *avant que* (but not *après que*) | before |
| *de crainte que, de peur que* | for fear that |
| *sans que* | without |
| *malgré que* | even though, in spite of |
| *pour autant que* | as far as |

## Conjunctions That DO NOT Take the Subjunctive

| | |
|---|---|
| *après que* | after |
| *dès que, aussitôt que* | as soon as |
| *pendant que* | during |
| *parce que* | because |
| *puisque* | since |
| *étant donné que* | given that / with the understanding that |
| *tandis que* | while / whereas |

## So Now What?

You won't have to construct the subjunctive of a given verb; you only need to recognize it among the four answer choices. In addition to the present subjunctive, you may also see the past of the subjunctive. You'll recognize it because the auxiliary or helper verb (*avoir* or *être*) will be in the subjunctive. Note that with avoir, *il a* becomes *il ait* and with être, *il est* becomes *il soit*.

## Present Tense

*Certain:*  *Je sais qu'il vient ce soir.*
I know that he is coming tonight.

*Uncertain:*  *Je doute qu'il vienne ce soir.*
(Pres. Subj.)  I doubt that he is coming tonight.

# Past Tense

Certain:        *Je sais qu'il est venu hier.*
                                    I know that he came yesterday.

Uncertain:    *Je doute qu'il soit venu hier.*
(Past Subj.)      I doubt that he came yesterday.

Now you try it:

_____⊘_____

Jean-Paul ne m'a pas téléphoné; j'ai peur qu'il
------- oublié notre rendez-vous.

(A) a
(B) avait
(C) ait
(D) aura

## Here's How to Crack It

Does the expression *J'ai peur que* . . . take the subjunctive? Yes! It shows doubt, fear, or uncertainty. The answer is (C).

_____⊘_____

Try another one:

_____⊘_____

Ma mère m'a grondée quand elle ------- ma robe déchirée.

(A) voit
(B) a vu
(C) voie
(D) ait vu

## Here's How to Crack It

Does the expression *Ma mère m'a grondée quand* . . . take the subjunctive?

No. The verb in this case (*voir*) is an actual event. Eliminate (C) and (D). This sentence requires the past, so the answer is (B). Also, note that we have *quand* here and not *que*.

_____⊘_____

Détruisez les preuves avant qu'il n'------- ce que nous avons fait.

(A) apprendra
(B) apprenne
(C) apprendrait
(D) apprend

### Here's How to Crack It

Is *avant que* a conjunction that takes the subjunctive?

Yes. The answer is (B). (A) is the future. (C) is the conditional. (D) is the present.

# Tense

You remember all those fancy verb tenses you learned in French class: the *passé simple*, the future perfect, the pluperfect subjunctive? Well, for the purposes of this test, you can forget them.

For the SAT French, you need to recognize the present, the imperfect, the *passé composé*, the *plus-que-parfait*, the future, the conditional, the past of the conditional, and you must know when to use them. The subjunctive, actually a mode or mood rather than a tense, is the verb form most frequently tested. The conditional, also a mode or mood, is the next most frequently tested verb form.

## Le Présent

This is pretty straightforward. It's the form of the verb you're most used to seeing.

*Il part.*

## L'Imparfait

The imperfect tense is a form of the past that indicates something was ongoing: either something that went on for a period of time in the past or something that happened repeatedly in the past.

| *présent* | *imparfait* |
|---|---|
| *Il part.* | *Il partait.* |

## Le Passé Composé

**The *Passé Composé* vs. the *Imparfait***
Notice the difference between the *passé composé* and the *imparfait*. The *passé composé* describes a one-time action that is now complete, while the *imparfait* describes an action that was ongoing in the past.

This tense indicates that a past action (or state) is now complete. It is made up of an auxiliary verb (either *avoir* or *être* in the present tense) and a past participle. It indicates something that started and ended in the past and is now over.

| *présent* | *passé composé* |
|---|---|
| *Il part.* | *Il est parti.* |

## Le Plus-Que-Parfait (Past Imperfect)

The past imperfect indicates that something happened in the past prior to another action in the past. It is made up of an auxiliary verb (*avoir* or *être* in the imperfect tense) and a past participle.

| *présent* | *plus-que-parfait* |
|---|---|
| *Il part.* | *Il était parti.* |

## Le Futur

This indicates that something will happen.

| *présent* | *futur* |
|---|---|
| *Il part.* | *Il partira.* |

## Le Conditionnel

The conditional is actually a mode or mood, not a tense. It is used to describe if/then situations.

The conditional mode or mood is used to describe what people would do or what would happen if a set of conditions were met. In most cases it is used with another clause starting with *si*.

| *présent* | *conditionnel* |
|---|---|
| *Il part.* | *Si cela arrivait, il partirait.* |
| | *Il partirait si cela arrivait.* |

The conditional is also used as a polite way to request things.

*Je voudrais une baguette, s'il vous plaît, madame.*
I would like a baguette please, madame.

## Use of the Conditional

Almost half of the questions that relate to verb sequence test you on the use of the conditional. The conditional is used in a sentence if there is a clause that begins with *si* and uses the imperfect tense.

*si + imparfait → conditionnel*

*Si j'avais le temps, je le ferais moi-même.*
> If I had the time, I would do it myself.

If the past imperfect is used, then the past conditional will be used.

*si + plus-que-parfait → conditionnel passé*

*Si j'avais eu le temps, je l'aurais fait moi-même.*
> If I had had the time, I would have done it myself.

You will use the conditional before or after clauses that start with *si* and contain the imperfect.

| | |
|---|---|
| *Présent* | *Aujourd'hui, il fait ses devoirs.* |
| *Imparfait* | *Quand il était petit, il faisait ses devoirs.* |
| *Passé composé* | *Hier il a fait ses devoirs.* |
| *Plus-Que-Parfait* | *J'avais déjà fini mes devoirs quand il est parti.* |
| *Futur* | *Demain, il fera ses devoirs.* |
| *Conditionnel* | *S'il avait des devoirs, il les ferait.* |

## Sequence of Tenses

In questions with several verbs, the tenses and mode must follow a logical sequence.

- Sentences with a *si* clause:

| *Si* clause | Resuit |
|---|---|
| *impartfait* | *conditionnel présent* |
| *Si j'avais de l'argent* | *j'achèterais un bateau.* |
| *plus-que-parfait* | *conditionnel passé* |
| *Si j'avais eu de l'argent* | *j'aurais fait ce voyage en Afrique.* |

- Conjunctions referring to time such as *quand, une fois que, après que, lorsque, aussitôt que,* and *dès que* often require the use of the *futur antérieur* (future perfect) instead of the *futur simple*. You must consider whether:
  1. In the sequence of future events, one action must be finished before the other can take place.

     *Je pourrai répondre à ta question quand j'aurai parlé à mon frère.*
       I will be able to answer your question when I have talked to my brother.

  2. In the future, the actions in both clauses will take place at the same time.

     *Je vous appellerai quand il arrivera à la maison.*
       I will call you as soon as he arrives.

---

Je sortirai aussitôt que mon travail -------.

(A) finira
(B) serait fini
(C) sera fini
(D) finirait

### Here's How to Crack It

What tense is correct? It is not a *si* clause or any form of politeness; therefore, it cannot be conditional mode. Eliminate (B) and (D). The conjunction *aussitôt que* indicates that one action has to take place before the other. Eliminate (A). (C) is the correct answer.

---

Si j'étais riche, je ------- un yacht.

(A) m'achète
(B) m'achèterai
(C) m'achetais
(D) m'achèterais

### Here's How to Crack It

What tense is correct here? Because *si* is used with the imperfect, the following verb must be the conditional.

How do we recognize the conditional? It combines the structure of the future with the endings of the imperfect (*ais*, *ait*, etc.). (D) is the correct choice.

———————○———————

———————○———————

Avant d'entrer au restaurant, il m'a demandé si j'
------- assez d'argent pour payer le dîner.

(A) ai
(B) avais
(C) ai eu
(D) aurai

## Here's How to Crack It

What tense is correct here? (A) cannot be correct. It is the present tense, and the previous clause, *il m'a demandé*, tells us the action is in the past. Since (D) is the future, we can eliminate it as well.

Do we use the imperfect or the past? (C) implies that having enough money was an event or action that occurred once prior to the question. Because we have the phrase, *avant d'entrer*, we know that the state of having money is an ongoing one, preceding and presumably continuing throughout dinner. (B) is the correct answer.

———————○———————

Make sure you can identify which tense (or mood) is which.

> It is important that you recognize what each tense or mood looks like when you see it. Usually the ending of the verb will give you a clue.

| Présent | Imparfait | Passé composé | Plus-que-parfait |
|---|---|---|---|
| *je donne* | *je donnais* | *j'ai donné* | *j'avais donné* |
| *tu donnes* | *tu donnais* | *tu as donné* | *tu avais donné* |
| *il donne* | *il donnait* | *il a donné* | *il avait donné* |
| *nous donnons* | *nous donnions* | *nous avons donné* | *nous avions donné* |
| *vous donnez* | *vous donniez* | *vous avez donné* | *vous aviez donné* |
| *ils donnent* | *ils donnaient* | *ils ont donné* | *ils avaient donné* |

| Futur | Conditionnel | Subjonctif présent | Conditionnel passé |
|---|---|---|---|
| *je donnerai* | *je donnerais* | *que je donne* | *j'aurais donné* |
| *tu donneras* | *tu donnerais* | *que tu donnes* | *tu aurais donné* |
| *il donnera* | *il donnerait* | *qu'il donne* | *il aurait donné* |
| *nous donnerons* | *nous donnerions* | *que nous donnions* | *nous aurions donné* |
| *vous donnerez* | *vous donneriez* | *que vous donniez* | *vous auriez donné* |
| *ils donneront* | *ils donneraient* | *qu'ils donnent* | *ils auraient donné* |

With *donner*, as in all regular "*er*" verbs, the singular forms of the subjunctive present are identical to the indicative present.

# AVOIR AND ÊTRE IN COMPOUND PAST TENSES

## What Is an Auxiliary Verb?

It is a verb that loses its own meaning to help form a compound past tense for other verbs such as the *passé composé, plus-que-parfait, passé du subjonctif, conditionnel passé,* and *futur antérieur.* Some verbs take either *avoir* or *être.* To make a sweeping generalization, **most verbs take *avoir***, but verbs that indicate a **change of place** (*aller, venir, partir*) **or state** (*naître, mourir, devenir…*) **and all reflexive verbs** (*se laver, se lever…*) take *être.* Sound tricky? Just remember Dr. and Mrs. Vandertramp.

Meet your new BFFs, Dr. and Mrs. Vandertramp!

You're probably familiar with the avoir vs. etre auxiliary verb divide from French class, but let's review just in case. When you are writing a sentence in passe compose, you must use either avoir or etre as your helper verb before the past participle. Most of the time, the auxiliary verb that you'll use is avoir ("to have") but sometimes it will be etre ("to be"). To help you remember what verbs pair up with etre, let me introduce you to my trusted friends, Dr. and Mrs. Vandertramp. Who are Dr. and Mrs. Vandertramp? They're a couple that every French student should know, even if doctors make you anxious. Memorize that pneumonic and it will help you recall a list of the verbs that use etre as their auxiliary verb in passé compose:

| | | | |
|---|---|---|---|
| Devenir | to become | Venir | to come |
| Revenir | to come back | Aller | to go |
| & | | Naître | to be born |
| Monter | to climb | Descendre | to go down |
| Rester | to stay | Entrer | to enter |
| Sortir | to go out | Rentrer | to come back |
| | | Tomber | to fall |
| | | Retourner | to return |
| | | Arriver | to arrive |
| | | Mourir | to die |
| | | Partir | to leave |

## What Is a Past Participle?

A past participle is the form of the verb that combines with "to have" (in English), or *être* or *avoir* (in French), in order to make the past tense.

*Je mange mon petit déjeuner.*    *J'ai **mangé** mon petit déjeuner.*
 I eat my breakfast. (present)    I have eaten my breakfast. (past)

You'll most likely be given the choice of four different forms of the past participle—masculine singular, feminine singular, masculine plural, and feminine plural—with an occasional infinitive thrown in to confuse you. You must decide which is correct.

## When Does the Past Participle Agree, and with What?

The past participle **agrees with the subject** of the sentence when:

- The verb takes *être* as its auxiliary verb and there is **no direct object placed after the verb.**

    *Pauline et Chantal sont parties hier pour l'Afrique.*
    Pauline and Chantal left for Africa yesterday.

- The verb is **reflexive** and therefore takes *être,* and there is **no direct object.**

    *Elle s'est évanouie quand elle a entendu la nouvelle.*
    She fainted when she heard the news.

The past participle **agrees with the direct object** of the sentence when:

- The **reflexive** verb has a **direct object placed before the verb.**

    *La jambe qu'elle s'est cassée en skiant lui fait toujours mal.*
    The leg she broke skiing is still painful.

- The verb takes *avoir* and has a **direct object placed before the verb.**

    *La fille que nous avons vue au café est ma meilleure amie.*
    The girl we saw in the café is my best friend.

## When Is There No Agreement?

- The **reflexive** verb has a **direct object** (usually a body part) **placed after the verb.**

    *Elle s'est piqué le doigt en cousant.*
    She pricked her finger while sewing.

    *Elle s'est lavé les cheveux ce matin.*
    She washed her hair this morning.

- The verb takes *avoir* and has a **direct object placed after the verb.**

    *J'ai vu ma meilleure amie au café aujourd'hui.*
    I saw my best girlfriend in the café today.

Since questions in Part C often contain several sentences, information about the gender and number may come earlier than the sentence in which the blank appears.

The past participle will agree with the *subject* if the verb takes *être* or is reflexive.
It will agree with the *object* of the sentence if the verb takes *avoir* and the direct object is before the verb.

Try this:

---○---

Les deux sœurs ont très bien ------- à l'université.

(A) réussi
(B) réussie
(C) réussis
(D) réussies

### Here's How to Crack It
The verb *réussir* (to succeed, to be successful) uses the auxiliary verb *avoir*. Is there a direct object that precedes the verb? No. There is no direct object in this sentence. The correct answer is (A).

---○---

---○---

La fille à côté de moi m'a donné les
renseignements dont j'avais besoin. Je l'ai ------.

(A) remercié
(B) remerciée
(C) remerciées
(D) remercier

### Here's How to Crack It
The verb *remercier* (to thank) also takes *avoir* as its helper verb. Is there a direct object before the verb? Yes, "*l*" refers to *la fille*. The correct answer is (B).

---○---

# Oddball Verb Forms: Other Participles

There is a small chance that you will have a question or two on other participles: the present participle, the gerund, or the perfect participle. You don't need to know these terms—just be able to recognize how they work in a sentence. This type of question is most likely to appear on Part C, where you choose the appropriate form of the verb based on the sequence of tenses in the paragraph.

## The Present Participle

The present participle is a verb form that ends in "-ing" in English. It shows that one action is happening at the same time as another.

> *J'ai vu les enfants courant sur la pelouse.*
> I saw the children running on the lawn.

The present participle "running" is also acting as an adjective, describing something about the children.

## The Gerund

The gerund is also like an "-ing" verb form in English, but in this case, it is acting as a noun rather than an adjective. In French, it is always accompanied by the preposition *en*. It can show:

- **That one action is happening at the same time as another**

  *Elle montait l'escalier en chantant.*
  She climbed the stairs while singing.

- **That one action is part of a process**

  *En lisant, nous découvrons de nouveaux mondes.*
  In reading, we discover new worlds.

- **That one action is part of a cause and effect**

  *Eric apprend à danser en regardant des vidéos.*
  Eric learns how to dance by watching videos.

## The Perfect Participle

The perfect participle (made up of *ayant* or *étant* + the past participle) is the past tense of the present participle. An example in English would be "Having won the war, the army celebrated." This form is used to show that one action was completed before another began.

> ***Ayant fini*** *le repas, nous avons débarrassé la table.*
> Having finished the meal, we cleared the table.

If the verb takes *être*, you will see *étant* instead of *ayant*:

> ***Étant montée****, elle ne pouvait plus entendre la discussion.*
> Having gone upstairs, she could no longer hear the discussion.

Since you're an expert by now, let's try tackling a full paragraph:

---

Hier, j'étais en train de ----(1)---- la maison quand j'ai vu à travers la fenêtre un lapin sur la pelouse. Son corps ----(2)---- brun, mais il avait des grandes oreilles blanches. Je l'----(3)---- regardé pendant quelques instants, puis en entendant un bruit il a ----(4)---- et en un clin d'œil il a disparu.

1. (A) rouler
   (B) ranger
   (C) nager
   (D) hausser

2. (A) est
   (B) a été
   (C) serais
   (D) était

3. (A) aie
   (B) ai
   (C) aura
   (D) aurais

4. (A) choisi
   (B) établi
   (C) bondi
   (D) dormi

### Here's How to Crack It

1. Which verb describes something that can be done in a house (*maison*)? *Rouler* means to roll, *ranger* means to tidy up, *nager* means to swim, and *hausser* means to raise. Only (B) makes sense in this context.

2. Which form of the verb *être* is correct here? Since the entire paragraph takes place in the past, we can eliminate both the present tense in (A), *est*, and the conditional in (C), *serais*. Now we have to choose between the *passé composé* in (B) or the imperfect in (D). Because the sentence is describing specific characteristics of the rabbit (*lapin*), we need to use the imperfect, which is used to describe states of being that are ongoing. The fact that the other verb in the sentence is also imperfect (*avait*) is another hint that (D), *était*, is the right answer.

3. Which form of the verb *avoir* is correct here? Again, all action is taking place in the past, and the other verbs in the sentence both appear to use the *passé composé*. Eliminate the future, (C), and the conditional, (D). In (A) we have the subjunctive form, but since there isn't any uncertainty or emotion here, it's incorrect, which leaves (B) as the correct answer.

4. Which past participle has the correct meaning for the sentence? Translating the second half of the sentence, we learn that upon hearing a noise (*en entendant un bruit*), it (the rabbit) does something and in the blink of an eye, it disappears (*en un clin d'œil il a disparu*). (A) means the rabbit chose something, which doesn't fit. (B) doesn't work either, as the rabbit didn't establish anything. (C) is the past participle of *bondir*, which means to leap; this would be a logical thing for the rabbit to do. (D) suggests the rabbit slept, which isn't correct. (C) is the right answer.

---

# DRILL 2: VERB QUESTIONS

Answers can be found in Part III.

1. Si -------, je préparerais le dîner.

   (A) vous en avez envie
   (B) on me le demande
   (C) j'avais le temps
   (D) tu seras d'accord

2. Paul regrette que nous ------- pas réussi.

   (A) n'avons
   (B) n'avions
   (C) n'ayons
   (D) n'aurons

3. ------- une lettre quand on a sonné à la porte.

(A) J'écris
(B) J'écrirais
(C) J'écrive
(D) J'écrivais

4. Elle n'a jamais oublié ce que nous -------
au moment de son départ.

(A) disons
(B) ayons dit
(C) avons dit
(D) aurions dit

5. Est-ce que vous ------- contents si je n'avais pas
accepté l'invitation?

(A) êtes
(B) soyez
(C) étiez
(D) auriez été

6. Nous doutons ------- leur rendre visite chez eux.

(A) qu'il ait le temps de
(B) qu'il voudrait
(C) qu'il peut
(D) qu'elle avait envie de

7. -------, elle est partie pour le long trajet chez elle.

(A) Disait au revoir
(B) Dire au revoir
(C) Ayant dit au revoir
(D) Avoir dit au revoir

8. Tu pourras regarder la télé une fois que tu ---------
ton travail.

(A) aurais fini
(B) finissais
(C) auras fini
(D) finisses

# PREPOSITIONS

Below is a list of the most important prepositions for you to know.

| Common Prepositions | |
|---|---|
| *à* | = to |
| *de* | = from, of |
| *sur* | = on |
| *sous* | = under |
| *pour* | = for |
| *avant (+ nom)* | = before |
| *avant de (+ verbe)* | = before |
| *après* | = after |
| *chez* | = at, to (location) |
| *en* | = of, in, from, to |
| *dans* | = in, into |
| *entre* | = between |
| *pendant* | = during |
| *vers* | = toward |
| *sans* | = without |
| *sauf* | = except, unless |
| *selon* | = according to |
| *durant* | = during |
| *malgré, en dépit de* | = in spite of |
| *afin de* | = in order to |

Just as in English, certain verbs or expressions in French require prepositions while others require none. Memorization is the key here.

These questions will ask you for the preposition required. Some verbs can take more than one preposition depending on the meaning. In some questions, you will have the option of no preposition, denoted by a dash in the answer choice (—).

Il a refusé ------- faire son lit.

(A) ---
(B) à
(C) de
(D) sur

Out of context, *refuser* could take the preposition *à* or *de*, or no preposition at all. Each has a different meaning.

*refuser quelque chose*—to refuse something

> *Il a refusé l'offre.*
> > He refused the offer.

*refuser quelque chose à quelqu'un*—to deny something to someone

> *Le juge a refusé les droits de visite à la mère.*
> > The judge denied visitation rights to the mother.

*refuser de faire quelque chose*—to refuse to do something

> *L'enfant a refusé de manger ses carottes.*
> The child refused to eat her carrots.

> Prepositions are tested on Parts A and B of your SAT French Subject Test. As parts of grammar, prepositions join words and have specific meanings, and certain verbs can be used only with certain prepositions (also known as "idioms").

Which is appropriate for this question? Because someone is refusing to do something in this sentence, the correct answer is *de*, choice (C).

## Back to Pronouns

Keep in mind that the verb's appropriate preposition may determine your choice of pronoun. If a verb requires a preposition in a given circumstance, for example, then you know that it takes an indirect and not a direct object. Or, if a given verb requires *de*, the relative pronoun used with it will reflect that.

---

C'est la robe ------- j'ai envie.

(A) que
(B) qui
(C) dont
(D) à qui

### Here's How to Crack It

The verb *avoir envie* takes the preposition *de*. (A) can be eliminated because *que* is never used with a preposition. (B) can also be eliminated because *qui* cannot be a subject here (*j'* is the subject). *Avoir envie* takes *de*, so (D), which is used with *à*, cannot be right. (C) *dont* is correct because *dont* in a sense means *de* + *que*.

---

> Your knowledge of prepositions will affect your choice of pronouns. For example, *dont* will be a correct choice only if the verb takes *de* as a preposition.

Your experience studying French will probably provide you with a good sense of which verb takes which preposition, if you take the time to think about it. To refresh your memory, here is a partial list of verbs. Some never take a preposition, others sometimes take a preposition, and still others always take a preposition.

## Verbs That Don't Take a Preposition

Verbs that don't take prepositions will be used with either the infinitive (the "to" form of a verb) or a direct object. Some verbs can be used with both.

| | |
|---|---|
| *pouvoir* + **infinitive** | *Je peux faire n'importe quoi.*<br>I can do anything I want. |
| *espérer* + **infinitive** | *J'espère venir demain.*<br>I hope to come tomorrow. |
| *vouloir* + **infinitive** | *Je veux chanter.*<br>I want to sing. |
| *vouloir* + **object** | *Je veux cette chemise.*<br>I want this shirt. |
| *mettre* + **object** | *Il a mis le vase sur la table.*<br>He put the vase on the table. |
| *faire* + **object** | *Marie a fait la vaisselle.*<br>Marie washed the dishes. |
| *acheter* + **object** | *Il a acheté trois pantalons.*<br>He bought three pairs of pants. |

## Verbs That Sometimes Take Prepositions and Sometimes Don't

| | |
|---|---|
| *aller* + **infinitive** | *Je vais chercher ma sœur à l'école.*<br>I am going to get my sister at school. |
| *aller à* | *Je vais aux États-Unis.*<br>I am going to the United States. |
| *refuser* + **object** | *Je refuse l'offre.*<br>I refuse the offer. |

A good resource to have on hand is a verb book. A good verb book will tell you how to conjugate a given verb and which prepositions are used with that verb.

| | |
|---|---|
| *refuser de* | *Je refuse de faire mes devoirs.* |
| | I refuse to do my homework. |
| *oublier* + noun | *J'ai oublié mon stylo.* |
| | I forgot my pen. |
| *oublier de* | *J'ai oublié de dire au revoir.* |
| | I forgot to say good-bye. |
| *accepter* + object | *J'accepte votre invitation.* |
| | I accept your invitation. |
| *accepter de* | *J'accepte de nettoyer la cuisine.* |
| | I agree to clean the kitchen. |
| *compter* + object | *Je compte ma monnaie.* |
| | I am counting my change. |
| *compter sur* | *Nous comptons sur vous pour nous aider.* |
| | We count on you to help us. |

## Verbs That Always Take Prepositions

| | |
|---|---|
| *réfléchir à* | *Je réfléchis à mon avenir.* |
| | I am thinking of my future. |
| *penser à* | *Je pense à ma mère.* |
| | I am thinking of my mother. |
| *penser de* | *Que pensez-vous du nouveau président?* |
| | What do you think of (about) the new president? |
| *participer à* | *Je participe aux Jeux Olympiques.* |
| | I am in the Olympic games. |
| *assister à* | *Est-ce que vous allez assister au concert?* |
| | Are you going to attend the concert? |
| *faire attention à* | *Faites attention aux assiettes en porcelaine!* |
| | Be careful with the porcelain plates! |

| | |
|---|---|
| *répondre à* | *Les élèves répondent aux questions du professeur.* |
| | The students answer the teacher's questions. |
| | |
| *obéir à* | *Le soldat obéit aux ordres.* |
| | The soldier obeys the orders. |
| | |
| *parler de* | *De quoi parlez-vous? Du chat?* |
| | What are you talking about? About the cat? |
| | |
| *avoir peur de* | *J'ai peur des araignées.* |
| | I am afraid of spiders. |
| | |
| *risquer de* | *Il risque de tomber.* |
| | He may fall. |
| | |
| *venir de* | *Je viens du supermarché.* |
| | I come from the supermarket. |
| | |
| *avoir envie de* | *J'ai envie d'un café.* |
| | I feel like having a coffee. |
| | |
| *avoir besoin de* | *J'ai besoin d'un crayon pour écrire.* |
| | I need a pencil to write. |

## Set Expressions

Certain rules govern the use of some prepositions.

## When Discussing Going to a Country:

*Je passe mes vacances . . .*

Use *en* for feminine, singular countries.

*en France*
*en Italie*

Use *au* (*à* + *le*) for masculine, singular countries.

*au Canada*
*au Brésil*

Use *aux* (*à* + *les*) for multi-state countries, whether feminine or masculine.

*aux États-Unis*
*aux Bermudes*

## When Discussing Being in or Going to a Town or City:

*Je reste . . .*
*Je vais . . .*

### Use *à*:

*à Paris*
*à New York*
*à Londres*

## When Discussing Coming from a Country or Town:

*Il est venu . . .*

### Use *de* or *des* for feminine countries.

*de Russie*
*d'Allemagne*
*des Bermudes*

### Use *du* or *des* for masculine countries.

*du Japon*
*des États-Unis*

### Use *de* for all towns.

*de Paris*
*de Lyon*

| List of Some Countries with Their Genders | | |
|---|---|---|
| **Feminine** | **Masculine** | **Multi-State** |
| *la Russie* | *le Canada* | *les États-Unis (masc.)* |
| *la France* | *le Japon* | *les Pays-Bas (masc.)* |
| *l'Italie* | *le Brésil* | *les Bermudes (fem.)* |
| *l'Autriche* | *le Maroc* | *les Bahamas (fem.)* |
| *l'Allemagne* | *le Pérou* | *les Philippines (fem.)* |
| *la Belgique* | *le Viêt-Nam* | |
| *la Grèce* | *le Luxembourg* | |
| *la Roumanie* | *le Mexique* | |
| *l'Espagne* | *le Chili* | |
| *l'Angleterre* | *Le Liban* | |
| *l'Algérie* | *Le Sénégal* | |

## Use of *en* and *de* + Name of Materials

To describe the material an object is made of, use either *de* or *en* + the name of the material.

| | |
|---|---|
| *un sac en cuir* | a leather purse |
| *un pot de terre* | an earthenware pot |
| *un mur de pierre* | a stone wall |
| *un pantalon en velours côtelé* | corduroy pants |
| *un collier de diamants* | a diamond necklace |
| *un bracelet en argent* | a silver bracelet |
| *une maison en brique* | a brick house |
| *une chaise en bois* | a wooden chair |
| *un fil de fer* | a wire |

## Adverbs

You will want to be able to recognize French adverbs and not get confused by their various forms.

In English, most adverbs are formed with an adjective + the suffix **–ly**.

In French, most adverbs are formed with the feminine form of the adjective and the suffix *–ment*.

| | | |
|---|---|---|
| *active* | → | *activement* |
| *ponctuelle* | → | *ponctuellement* |
| *calme* | → | *calmement* |

When the adjectives end with *–i, –ai, –u,* and *–é,* the adverbs are formed with the masculine form of the adjective.

| | | |
|---|---|---|
| *vrai* | → | *vraiment* |
| *assidu* | → | *assidûment* |
| *poli* | → | *poliment* |

When the adjectives end with *–ant* or *–ent,* the endings of the adverbs change to *–mment.*

| | | |
|---|---|---|
| *prudent* | → | *prudemment* |
| *négligent* | → | *négligemment* |
| *savant* | → | *savamment* |

Also remember that some irregular adverbs are different from the adjectives:

| | | |
|---|---|---|
| *bon* | → | *bien* |
| *rapide* | → | *vite* |

*meilleur* → *mieux*
*mauvais* → *mal*

Be aware of certain adverbs placed as attributive adjectives. They do not agree with the nouns, of course, but you might mistakenly think they need to be eliminated because of their position in the sentence. Take a look at a few examples:

*Il y a encore des places debout dans la salle de spectacle.*
*Mettez les bagages dans les coffres arrière.*
*Les roues avant sont à changer.*

# DRILL 3: PREPOSITION QUESTIONS

Answers can be found in Part III.

1. Marie ------- les résultats de ses examens.

   (A) pense
   (B) attend
   (C) compte
   (D) a envie

2. Je ------- de leur écrire.

   (A) suis obligé
   (B) espère
   (C) veux
   (D) réfléchis

3. Je n'ai jamais eu l'occasion ------- voir ce film.

   (A) ---
   (B) à
   (C) de
   (D) sur

4. ------- le concert, elles bavardaient sans cesse.

   (A) Pendant
   (B) Dans
   (C) Avec
   (D) En

5. Je la vois souvent à -------.

   (A) France
   (B) ville
   (C) la boulangerie
   (D) loin

6. Elle n'a pas réfléchi ------- de refuser l'offre.

   (A) ---
   (B) avant
   (C) après
   (D) à

# ODDS AND ENDS

At most, these topics will come up once or twice on the test.

Odds and ends are just that: small, picky questions that show up from time to time but don't appear on every test.

## Adjective Versus Adverb

Adjectives modify nouns. Adverbs modify verbs, adjectives, and other adverbs. In French, adverbs often end in *-ment*.

> Elle a remplacé le vase -------.
>
> (A) doux
> (B) brusquement
> (C) difficile
> (D) ennuyeuse

(A), (C), and (D) are all adjectives. (B) is the right answer.

When modifying an adjective, use the adverbs *trop*, *plus*, *très*, *si*, or *moins*.

*Mieux*, like *pire*, cannot be used to modify an adjective.

> Ce cassoulet est ------- bon.
>
> (A) mieux
> (B) sans
> (C) si
> (D) pas

*Bon* is an adjective. The word in the blank must be an adverb. Only *si* is an adverb that can be used to modify an adjective. (C) is the right answer.

## Active Versus Passive

If you use *être* with the past participle of a verb that normally takes *avoir*, you are forming the passive tense of the verb.

| Active (present) | Passive (present) |
|---|---|
| *Le facteur distribue le courrier.* | *Le courrier est distribué par le facteur.* |
| The postman delivers the mail. | The mail is delivered by the postman. |

## Possessive Adjectives

Possessive adjectives (not pronouns) show that a given noun belongs to a given person. But, unlike in English, French possessive adjectives agree with the gender and number of what is owned, not who owns it. The form of the adjective also changes depending on whether the noun begins with a vowel or a silent "h."

*Son* is the masculine singular and *sa* is the feminine singular. However, if a feminine noun begins with a vowel or a silent "h," the possessive adjective that goes with it will be *son*. *Sa* does not shorten to s'.

> Elle avait de la soupe dans ------- assiette.
>
> (A) son
> (B) sa
> (C) s'
> (D) ses

Is *assiette* masculine or feminine? Singular or plural?

*Assiette* is feminine, but the word begins with a vowel; you can't say *sa assiette*, so eliminate (B). Possessive adjectives don't contract, so eliminate (C). *Assiette* is singular; cancel (D), which is plural. (A) is the right answer.

Even though *amie* is feminine, you <u>can't</u> say *sa amie* or *s'amie*. When you have a feminine noun that begins with a vowel, it will take the masculine version of the possessive adjective—in this case, *son amie*. The College Board loves to ask this kind of question.

| | Only one object | | More than one object |
|---|---|---|---|
| | *masculin* | *féminin* | *masculin et féminin* |
| **One owner** | *mon livre* | *ma cravate* | *mes sœurs* |
| | *ton frère* | *ta santé* | *tes vacances* |
| | *son amie* | *sa voiture* | *ses cheveux* |
| | *masculin et féminin* | | *masculin et féminin* |
| **More than one owner** | *notre professeur* | | *nos vœux* |
| | *votre chemise* | | *vos souhaits* |
| | *leur voiture* | | *leurs cahiers* |

# SPECIAL POINTS FOR PART C

## 1. Is It Vocabulary or Grammar?

How can you tell? **A vocabulary question** will have **four words with clearly different meanings**. **A grammar question** will usually have **one word in four different forms** (for example, the same verb in four different tenses or with four different prepositions). When you see practice examples, the difference will be obvious.

## 2. Think of the Paragraph as a Whole

The paragraph is telling a story, so all sentences are connected. The key to this section is realizing that the correct answer can be based on both the sentence with the blank and on the sentences that precede it. You may even need to read past the blank sometimes in order to get a better understanding of what's going on. **Don't think of each sentence as a separate question.**

## 3. Special Grammar Points

Some grammatical points are tested more frequently in Part C than in Part B. All the following points are thoroughly discussed earlier in this chapter.

### Verb Sequence

The **action** described in the paragraph must unfold **in a logical sequence. Make sure all the verbs** that you choose as answers **match the tense of the story.** Pay special attention to the rules for use of the imperfect and the conditional.

### Agreement of the Past Participle

As we discussed earlier in this chapter, a past participle will agree with the *subject* if the verb takes *être*. If the verb takes *avoir* and the direct object comes before the verb, it will agree with the *object* of the sentence. In some cases, whether the direct object is masculine or feminine is revealed in a previous sentence.

## SUMMARY

Questions in Parts B and C of the SAT French Subject Test evaluate your ability to choose correct words or expressions based on your understanding of French grammar. Here are the main grammar points you should review before the test:

There are two kinds of pronoun questions on the test: one asks you to choose among the five main kinds of pronouns (subject, direct object, reflexive, indirect object, and stressed), and the other asks you to choose among pronouns like *qui, que, dont,* and *lequel.*

# Pronouns

Check which pronoun should be used in the sentence. Is it subject, direct object, reflexive, indirect object, or stressed? How about demonstrative, interrogative, relative, indefinite, or even another type of pronoun?

- Check its gender and number if needed (masculine, feminine, plural).
- Check whether it is also replacing a preposition.
- Check where it is placed in the sentence relative to the verb.

# Verbs

Can you figure out the tense or mode, the use of the auxiliary verb, the agreement with the past participle, the tense sequence, or the specific use of certain verbs?

- Check the subject of the sentence.
- Check the tense sequence by looking at the meaning of the main clause.
- Check whether the verb takes *être* or *avoir* in compound past tense.
- Look at prepositions and conjunctions to help you decide what verb form or mode you should use.

# Prepositions

Can you specify which one to use with which verb? What is the meaning when the preposition is combined with certain verbs and other words? How could it be replaced by a pronoun in a sentence?

- Check whether the verb takes *de* or *à.*
- Check whether the general meaning of the sentence indicates a place, a time, a cause, or something else.
- Check if the preposition is included in a pronoun form or if it should be transformed (*dont, auquel, duquel,* etc.).

# Adverbs

Can you see the difference between adjectives and adverbs?

- Check the word's position in the sentence.
- Check the ending of the word and memorize the irregular adverb forms so you don't get tricked.

# Comprehensive Drill

Answers can be found in Part III.

## Part B

**Directions:** Each of the following sentences contains a blank. From the four choices given, select the one that can be inserted in the blank to form a grammatically correct sentence. Choice (A) may consist of dashes that indicate that no insertion is required to form a grammatically correct sentence.

1. Marie a ------- à m'offrir.

   (A) quelque chose
   (B) rien
   (C) plusieurs
   (D) quelque

2. Claude ------- de faire les courses.

   (A) a rejeté
   (B) a aimé
   (C) est obligé
   (D) a voulu

3. C'est grâce à son ------- qu'il a réussi.

   (A) talents
   (B) amie
   (C) gentillesse
   (D) oncles

4. Je ferai la vaisselle -------.

   (A) avant de partir
   (B) à tout à l'heure
   (C) hier
   (D) jamais

5. C'est ------- qui a gagné!

   (A) personne
   (B) je
   (C) leur
   (D) elle

6. Nos voisins ------- aller à la piscine.

   (A) préfèrent
   (B) rêvent
   (C) plaisent
   (D) insistent

7. Je ------- demande s'il est temps de partir.

   (A) elle
   (B) moi
   (C) se
   (D) vous

8. Les dames sont arrivées avec -------.

   (A) leur
   (B) il
   (C) eux
   (D) les

9. La voiture verte est -------.

   (A) les leurs
   (B) la vôtre
   (C) à aucun
   (D) ma

10. L'année dernière j'ai voyagé en -------.

    (A) Russie
    (B) États-Unis
    (C) New York
    (D) Canada

11. La réussite de ce projet est -------.

   (A) certainement
   (B) peu
   (C) probable
   (D) malgré

12. ------- ce soit fini.

   (A) Nous savons que
   (B) Il regrette que
   (C) Elle a oublié que
   (D) C'est lui qui a décidé que

13. C'est le collègue ------- j'ai beaucoup parlé.

   (A) dont
   (B) de quoi
   (C) sauf qui
   (D) avant que

14. ------- est le metteur en scène de ce film?

   (A) Quelle
   (B) Qu'est-ce qui
   (C) Où
   (D) Quoi

15. ------- avez-vous envie?

   (A) Quel
   (B) Y
   (C) Dont
   (D) De quoi

16. Le gouvernement ------- de négocier un accord.

   (A) va
   (B) espère
   (C) essaie
   (D) peut

17. ------- qu'il sache les nouvelles d'hier.

   (A) Sans doute
   (B) Je sais
   (C) Je crains
   (D) C'est à cause de Michel

18. Jean a réussi à trouver du travail ------- la grève.

   (A) afin de
   (B) lorsque
   (C) en dépit de
   (D) à moins de

19. -------, nous partirions.

   (A) Si elle en avait envie
   (B) Si tu peux
   (C) S'ils voudront
   (D) Si vous l'aviez permis

20. C'est le gâteau le plus délicieux -------.

   (A) que vous avez jamais mangé
   (B) qu'elle a jamais acheté
   (C) que nous avons jamais fait
   (D) que tu puisses jamais imaginer

## Part C

**Directions:** The paragraphs below contain blank spaces indicating omissions in the text. For some blanks it is necessary to choose the completion that is most appropriate to the meaning of the passage; for other blanks, to choose the one completion that forms a grammatically correct sentence. In some instances, choice (A) may consist of dashes that indicate that no insertion is required to form a grammatically correct sentence. In each case, indicate your answer by filling in the corresponding oval on the answer sheet. Be sure to read each paragraph completely before answering the questions related to it.

Si j'avais su, ----(21)---- aller avec Marie et Christine. Trop tard, j'ai essayé de ----(22)---- téléphoner chez ----(23)---- mais ----(24)---- n'était là. ----(25)----, j'ai tenté de les retrouver au café. Quand ----(26)---- suis arrivé, je les ai ----(27)---- entrer ----(28)---- cinéma.

21. (A) je pouvais
    (B) j'avais pu
    (C) je peux
    (D) j'aurais pu

22. (A) elles
    (B) leur
    (C) eux
    (D) la

23. (A) elles
    (B) tu
    (C) leur
    (D) ils

24. (A) personne
    (B) une personne
    (C) rien
    (D) nulle

25. (A) Finalement
    (B) Terminé
    (C) Maintenant
    (D) Afin de

26. (A) j'en
    (B) j'y
    (C) je le
    (D) je me

27. (A) vu
    (B) vue
    (C) vus
    (D) vues

28. (A) à la
    (B) au
    (C) par la
    (D) par le

Avant ----(29)---- partir en vacances, Jean et Camille ont ----(30)---- à l'aéroport ----(31)---- demander ----(32)---- l'avion partait ----(33)----.

29. (A) ---
    (B) à
    (C) de
    (D) que

30. (A) téléphoné
    (B) téléphonée
    (C) téléphonés
    (D) téléphonées

31. (A) ---
    (B) à
    (C) de
    (D) pour

32. (A) si
    (B) quand
    (C) quel
    (D) qui

33. (A) en temps
    (B) chaque heure
    (C) à l'heure
    (D) de temps en temps

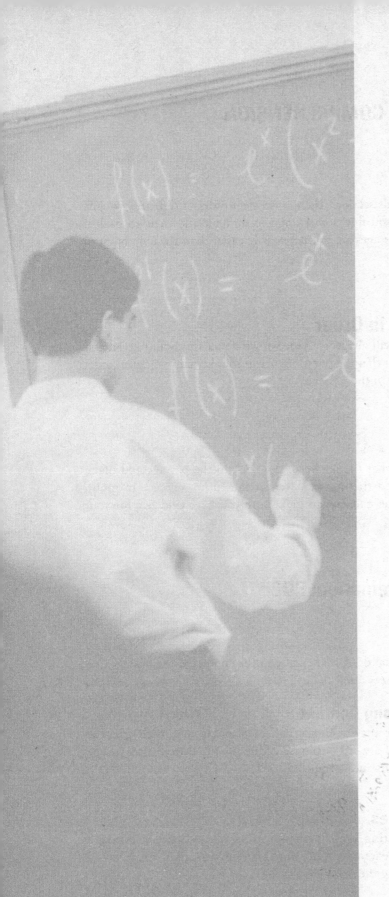

# Chapter 6
# Reading
# Comprehension

For Reading Comprehension, Part D of the SAT French Subject Test, you will have to read passages in French and answer critical questions.

You will have anywhere from 4 to 6 literary or journalistic passages, each about 20 to 30 lines. In addition, you may see 1 to 3 ticket/schedule/advertisement-type texts; these may or may not be accompanied by pictures.

There is no clear order of difficulty in this section, so you will have to use your judgment to determine which questions you are going to attempt first.

It is best to preview the questions first so you have a better sense of what to look for as you read the passages. The passages are generally quite short. Read them through at a moderate pace to get the general idea of what the passage is about. Do not become obsessed if you don't understand every word or sentence; however, keep an eye out for trap answers.

Get acquainted with the format of the test. Follow the suggestions we give you and then try the practice section at the end of this chapter.

# PART D: READING COMPREHENSION

## Pace Yourself

Do not be anxious about this section. There is no clear order of difficulty, so just go to the next question if you find something too difficult and then go back if you have time. The short passages are not necessarily easier than the long ones, so make sure you choose wisely.

## The Questions Are in Order

The questions on reading comprehension go in order of the text. The early questions relate to information early in the passage. Later questions refer to information that appears later in the passage.

Reading the questions first will give you an idea of what you are about to read and what to look for. Use the fact that the questions are in roughly chronological order to help you find the answers in the passage.

## Go Back

Once you have an idea of what the answer is, go back to the passage and make sure you are not falling for a trap answer. Reread the entire sentence or group of sentences that relate to the question to make sure you have evidence for your answer.

## Use Process of Elimination: POE

### Common Sense

You can eliminate answers that don't make sense in the context of the passage.

### Familiar Words—Wrong Context

Sometimes the words in an answer choice will be strongly reminiscent of the words used in the passage. If a word or phrase is directly lifted from the passage, be careful—you may be falling into a trap.

### Misleading Look-Alikes

Sometimes, instead of repeating words verbatim, the College Board will take a word and twist it subtly. For example, if the word *errer* appears, they might have a trap answer choice containing the word *erreur*.

# What Is This Weird Tense?

In formal French, literary writing uses a tense called the *passé simple* (or past historic) instead of the *passé composé*. You don't need to know how to conjugate it or when to use it. You simply need to recognize which verb is being used.

| Present | Past Participle | Passé Simple |
|---------|-----------------|--------------|
| il donne | donné | il donna |
| il croit | cru | il crut |
| il met | mis | il mit |

You should be able to recognize the *passé simple* forms of some commonly used French verbs, such as *aller, avoir, dire, être, faire, lire, mettre, pouvoir, prendre, savoir, venir, vouloir.*

Try the following passage, looking for the types of trap answers mentioned above.

---

## Part D

**Directions:** Read the following selections carefully for comprehension. Each selection is followed by a number of questions or incomplete statements. Select the completion or answer that is best according to the text and fill in the corresponding oval on the answer sheet.

La cité elle-même, on doit l'avouer, est laide.
*Ligne* D'aspect tranquille, il faut quelque temps pour
apercevoir ce qui la rend différente de tant
d'autres villes commerçantes, sous toutes les
5 latitudes. Comment faire imaginer, par exemple,
une ville sans pigeons, sans arbres et sans jardins,
où l'on ne rencontre ni battements d'ailes ni
froissements de feuilles, un lieu neutre pour tout
dire? Le changement des saisons ne s'y lit que
10 dans le ciel. Le printemps s'annonce seulement
par la qualité de l'air ou par les corbeilles de
fleurs que des petits vendeurs ramènent des banlieues; c'est un printemps qu'on vend sur les
marchés. Pendant l'été, le soleil incendie les mai-
15 sons trop sèches et couvre les murs d'une cendre
grise; on ne peut plus vivre alors que dans l'ombre
des volets clos. En automne, c'est, au contraire,

The best way to get the right answer is to take the time to go back and carefully reread the sentence or sentences that relate to the question.

un déluge de boue. Les beaux jours viennent seulement en hiver.
(Camus, *La Peste*, Folio)

1. Ce passage nous décrit

   (A) une ville idéale
   (B) un marché en ville
   (C) le changement des saisons
   (D) les attributs principaux d'une cité

2. Qu'est-ce qui rend la cité différente des autres villes?

   (A) la présence des pigeons
   (B) la latitude
   (C) le manque de verdure et d'oiseaux
   (D) la couleur du ciel

3. Aux lignes 13–14, "c'est un printemps qu'on vend sur les marchés" veut dire

   (A) qu'on peut tout acheter au marché
   (B) qu'on sait que le printemps est arrivé quand on peut acheter des fleurs
   (C) qu'on voit mieux le printemps dans les banlieues
   (D) que le printemps est comme un marché

4. Comment réagissent les habitants de la ville à l'arrivée de l'été?

   (A) Ils font des feux.
   (B) Ils se plaignent.
   (C) Ils restent à l'intérieur.
   (D) Ils deviennent des voleurs.

Don't be afraid to eliminate answer choices that don't make sense.

### Here's How to Crack It

1. Ce passage nous décrit

   (A) une ville idéale
   (B) un marché en ville
   (C) le changement des saisons
   (D) les attributs principaux d'une cité

You are asked to choose what the passage describes:

(A) "an ideal town" is a misunderstanding of the first sentence. The first sentence tells us that the city is ugly, and the passage goes on to list primarily negative qualities. Eliminate this choice.

(B) "a marketplace in town" is an example of familiar words / wrong context. The word *marché* appears, as does the word *vendeurs*; however, the passage as a whole is not about the market. This choice is too specific. Eliminate it.

(C) "the changing of the seasons" is another example of familiar words—wrong context. The change of seasons is discussed, but again, it is too specific for this question.

(D) **"the principal attributes of a town" is the correct answer.** The passage discusses several distinctive features of a city.

> 2. Qu'est-ce qui rend la cité différente des autres villes?
>
>    (A) la présence des pigeons
>    (B) la latitude
>    (C) le manque de verdure et d'oiseaux
>    (D) la couleur du ciel

You are asked to choose what makes the city different from other cities. The answer is in the section that starts with the second sentence of the passage.

(A) "the presence of pigeons" is an example of familiar words—wrong context. Pigeons are mentioned, but what is significant is their absence.

Watch out for answers that use familiar words from the passage out of context.

(B) "the latitude" is another example of familiar words—wrong context. The word "latitude" appears in the second sentence, but it is used to describe the location of other cities, in any latitude.

(C) **"the lack of greenery and birds" is the correct answer.** Notice that it paraphrases part of the third sentence: *sans pigeons, sans arbres et sans jardins.*

(D) "the color of the sky" takes the word *ciel* out of context. It is a misunderstanding of the sentence: *Le changement des saisons ne s'y lit que dans le ciel.*

> 3. Aux lignes 13–14, "c'est un printemps qu'on vend sur les marchés" veut dire
>
>    (A) qu'on peut tout acheter au marché
>    (B) qu'on sait que le printemps est arrivé
>        quand on peut acheter des fleurs
>    (C) qu'on voit mieux le printemps dans les
>        banlieues
>    (D) que le printemps est comme un marché

You are asked to interpret the sentence "it is a spring that is sold in the marketplace" within the context of the passage.

(A) "that one can buy everything at the market" is too literal and does not relate to the passage.

**(B) "that one knows spring has arrived when one can buy flowers" is the correct answer.** It corroborates the meaning, connecting it to the previous sentence about how few signs there are of the change of seasons.

(C) "that it is easier to see the spring in the suburbs" takes the word *banlieues* out of context.

(D) "that spring is like a marketplace" is a literal interpretation.

4. Comment réagissent les habitants de la ville à l'arrivée de l'été?

    (A) Ils font des feux.
    (B) Ils se plaignent.
    (C) Ils restent à l'intérieur.
    (D) Ils deviennent des voleurs.

"How do the inhabitants of the town react to the arrival of summer?" This topic is discussed in the third-to-last sentence of the passage.

(A) "They make fires" misinterprets the phrase *"le soleil incendie les maisons."*

(B) "They complain" comes out of the blue. Complaining is not discussed anywhere in the passage.

**(C) "They stay indoors" is the correct answer.** This is what the sentence *"on ne peut plus vivre alors que dans l'ombre des volets clos,"* implies—"then one can only live in the shade of closed shutters."

(D) "They become thieves" is an example of a misleading look-alike. Here the word *volets* (shutters) has been twisted into the word *voleurs*.

# TICKETS/SCHEDULES/ADVERTISEMENTS

These graphical passages can be a blessing because you have less to read and because common sense works so well. **Pay special attention to the small print.**

- Read through the schedule or advertisement.
- Get a sense of the layout. Read all sizes of print.
- Use your common sense.
- Eliminate misleading look-alike words.

---

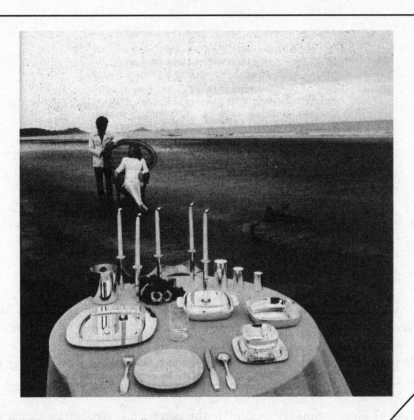

## les jeunes aiment l'argent

**Ils aiment l'argent signé Ravinet d'Enfert**
Ravinet d'Enfert a créé, en métal argenté, une collection contemporaine de qualité.
Héritier d'une longue tradition, éditeur d'une collection classique très réputée,
Ravinet d'Enfert propose des créations de notre temps comme
les services "Président" et "Brantôme." Ravinet d'Enfert les présente
avec des couverts, des plats, des luminaires et des accessoires de table
dans son catalogue "lignes actuelles."
Demandez-le dans les magasins ou à l'aide du bon à découper qui
se trouve à droite.

**RAVINET D'ENFERT**
**83, RUE DU TEMPLE—PARIS—3e**

Veuillez
m'adresser
gratuitement
vos catalogues
○ tradition
○ lignes actuelles

Nom _____

Prénom _____

Adresse _____

**The Small Print**
On ticket/schedule/advertisement-type questions, pay special attention to the small print and the titles!

1. Selon la publicité, les services "Président" et "Brantôme"

   (A) sont d'une collection classique
   (B) coûtent beaucoup d'argent
   (C) sont très réputés
   (D) sont d'un style contemporain

2. Le bon à découper vous offre

   (A) des produits gratuits
   (B) un choix de catalogues
   (C) des adresses
   (D) une description de nouvelles lignes

## Here's How to Crack It

1. Selon la publicité, les services "Président" et "Brantôme"

   (A) sont d'une collection classique
   (B) coûtent beaucoup d'argent
   (C) sont très réputés
   (D) sont d'un style contemporain

"According to the advertisement, the '*Président*' and '*Brantôme*' collections . . . "

(A) "are from a classic collection" takes a phrase out of context. The company produces a traditional line, but these styles, in contrast, are modern.

(B) "cost a lot of money" is also out of context. *Argent* is used here to mean "silver," not "money." This answer could be true, but there is no evidence of it in the ad.

(C) "have a good reputation" is also out of context. Again, the company is renowned, but we don't know about these specific lines.

(D) **"are of a contemporary design" is the correct answer.** Notice that it paraphrases the actual description *des créations de notre temps*.

2. Le bon à découper vous offre

   (A) des produits gratuits
   (B) un choix de catalogues
   (C) des adresses
   (D) une description de nouvelles lignes

"The coupon offers you . . . "

*Le bon à découper vous offre* refers to the coupon in the corner.

(A) "free products" is a familiar word, but it's in the wrong context. The catalog is free; the products are not.

**(B) "a choice of catalogs" is the correct answer.** The two boxes name two types of catalogs.

(C) "addresses" is a familiar word—wrong context. *Adresser* is part of a request to the company to send or address a catalog to the reader.

(D) "a description of new lines" is not terrible, but is not as good as choice (B). The coupon itself is not providing an actual description of the contemporary lines.

---

# Comprehensive Drill

Answers can be found in Part III.

## Part D

**Directions:** Read the following selections carefully for comprehension. Each selection is followed by a number of questions or incomplete statements. Select the completion or answer that is best according to the text and fill in the corresponding oval on the answer sheet.

Chez Rasseneur, après avoir mangé une soupe, Etienne, remonté dans l'étroite chambre qu'il allait occuper sous le toit, en face du Voreux, était tombé sur son lit, tout vêtu, assommé de fatigue. En deux jours, il n'avait pas dormi quatre heures. Quand il s'éveilla, au crépuscule, il resta étourdi un instant, sans reconnaître le lieu où il se trouvait; et il éprouvait un tel malaise, une telle pesanteur de tête, qu'il se mit péniblement debout, avec l'idée de prendre l'air, avant de dîner et de se coucher pour la nuit.
(Zola, *Germinal*, Garnier)

*Ligne*

5

1. Etienne n'avait pas l'énergie de

   (A) dormir
   (B) se déshabiller
   (C) manger
   (D) mettre ses habits

2. Selon le passage, pour quelle raison Etienne est-il fatigué?

   (A) Il a trop mangé.
   (B) Il n'a pas dormi du tout depuis deux jours.
   (C) Il s'est couché à quatre heures du matin.
   (D) Il n'a dormi que quelques heures en 48 heures.

3. A quel moment de la journée s'est-il réveillé?

   (A) tôt le matin
   (B) à midi
   (C) tôt le soir
   (D) à minuit

4. Comment réagit-il au moment de se réveiller?

   (A) Il ne se souvient pas où il est.
   (B) Il ne trouve pas ses habits.
   (C) Il se sent en retard.
   (D) Il a faim.

5. Que voulait-il faire avant de dîner?

   (A) respirer
   (B) se promener
   (C) s'éveiller
   (D) courir

Chaque dimanche, avant la guerre, Morissot partait dès l'aurore, une canne en bambou d'une main, une boîte en fer-blanc sur le dos. Il prenait le chemin de fer d'Argenteuil, descendait à Colombes, puis gagnait à pied l'île Marante. A peine arrivé en ce lieu de ses rêves, il se mettait à pêcher; il pêchait jusqu'à la nuit.

Chaque dimanche, il rencontrait là un petit homme replet et jovial, M. Sauvage, mercier, rue Notre-Dame-de-Lorette, un autre pêcheur fanatique. Ils passaient souvent une demi-journée à côté, la ligne à la main et les pieds ballants au-dessus du courant; et ils s'étaient pris d'amitié l'un pour l'autre.

(Guy de Maupassant, *Deux Amis*, Le Livre de Poche)

6. Quand Morissot partait-il pour l'île?

   (A) après le coucher du soleil
   (B) au moment du coucher du soleil
   (C) au moment du lever du soleil
   (D) l'après-midi

7. Comment gagnait-il l'île?

   (A) en autobus et à pied
   (B) en bateau
   (C) en voiture et à pied
   (D) en train et à pied

8. A quel moment commençait-il à pêcher?

   (A) pratiquement au moment où il arrivait
   (B) au moment où il commençait à rêver
   (C) à la tombée de la nuit
   (D) quand son ami arrivait

9. Qu'est-ce qui se trouvait dans la rue Notre-Dame-de-Lorette?

   (A) l'île Marante
   (B) l'endroit où les deux amis se rencontraient
   (C) le magasin de M. Sauvage
   (D) la gare

**Claire**.—Tes parents t'interdisent-ils d'aller voir un film?

**Guillaume**.—Non, puisque je leur demande ce qu'ils en pensent. Quelquefois, ils me disent: "Il vaut mieux que tu ailles voir un autre film."

**Claire**.—Moi, mes parents pensent qu'à mon âge, le cinéma n'est pas très bon, de toute façon.

**Gilles**.—Tu n'y vas jamais, alors?

**Claire**.—Si, mais en cachette.

**Guillaume**.—Ça alors, moi je ne le ferai jamais . . . Je ne peux pas mentir à mes parents. Je crois que je me sens libre parce que mes parents pensent que c'est un peu à moi de choisir, mais pas n'importe quoi.

(*Pour ou contre*, Hachette)

10. Les parents de Guillaume

    (A) lui conseillent de ne jamais aller au cinéma
    (B) ne sont pas concernés par ce qu'il fait
    (C) n'aiment pas le cinéma
    (D) lui donnent leur avis sur les films qu'il choisit

11. A la question de Gilles, Claire répond

    (A) qu'elle ne va jamais au cinéma
    (B) qu'elle va au cinéma si ses parents sont d'accord
    (C) qu'elle va au cinéma sans le dire à ses parents
    (D) qu'elle va souvent au cinéma

12. Quelle raison Guillaume donne-t-il pour ne pas mentir à ses parents?

    (A) Ses parents le laissent faire n'importe quoi.
    (B) Ses parents lui donnent la responsabilité de décider que faire.
    (C) Il vaut mieux ne pas le faire.
    (D) Ses parents n'aiment pas le cinéma.

Attention! Dans le 5e, le boulevard Saint-Michel et la place Saint-André-des-Arts ne sont plus fréquentables! Les petits bars sympathiques et les restaurants à petits prix ont disparu au profit d'établissements prétentieux où un personnel pressé sert des bières à la chaîne. On débite des sandwiches sous cellophane, des frites et, signe des temps, McDonald et Wimpy se font face, à deux pas du Luxembourg. Cinémas et librairies semblent résister, pour l'instant, à cette invasion "made in U.S." Les jeunes se pressent chez "Gibert" et dans les salles d'art et d'essai où passent les vieux films d'hier et ceux d'avant-garde. Pour se rencontrer, les jeunes préfèrent les petites rues plus anonymes, les petits restaurants à six ou sept tables, les bars sans faux clinquant que l'on trouve autour du Panthéon.
(*Paris*, Hachette)

*Ligne* 5, 10, 15 (line markers)

13. L'auteur réagit au changement sur le boulevard Saint-Michel et sur la place Saint-André-des-Arts avec

(A) impatience
(B) regret
(C) indifférence
(D) plaisir

14. Qu'est-ce qu'on trouve près du Luxembourg?

(A) des petits restaurants anonymes
(B) des cafés sympathiques
(C) des librairies prétentieuses
(D) des établissements américains

15. D'après le passage, on comprend que "Gibert" est

(A) un film
(B) un café
(C) une librairie
(D) un musée

16. Que font les jeunes au lieu d'aller au boulevard Saint-Michel?

(A) Ils fréquentent la place Saint-André-des-Arts.
(B) Ils sont pressés d'aller voir des films américains.
(C) Ils cherchent des bars sympathiques dans un autre endroit.
(D) Ils résistent à l'envie d'aller dans les librairies.

Je n'ai rien à cacher. J'étais orpheline et pauvre, j'élevais mon frère cadet. Un vieil ami de mon père m'a demandé ma main. Il était riche et bon, j'ai accepté. Qu'auriez-vous fait à ma place? Mon frère était malade et sa santé réclamait les plus grands soins. J'ai vécu six ans avec mon mari sans un nuage. Il y a deux ans, j'ai rencontré celui que je devais aimer. Nous nous sommes reconnus tout de suite, il voulait que je parte avec lui et j'ai refusé.
(Sartre, *Huis-clos*, Folio)

*Ligne* 5 (line markers)

17. La narratrice donne à entendre qu'elle

(A) travaillait beaucoup
(B) était invalide
(C) avait beaucoup de soucis
(D) s'était mariée avec l'ami de son père

18. Le frère de la narratrice

(A) a vécu avec elle pendant six ans
(B) était plus jeune qu'elle
(C) était soldat
(D) n'aimait pas son mari

19. Le passage nous donne l'impression

(A) qu'elle voulait défendre ses actions
(B) que son mari lui manquait
(C) que son frère était guéri
(D) qu'elle aimait le beau temps

20. Après six ans, qu'est-ce qui s'est passé?

(A) Le mari de la narratrice est parti.
(B) Le beau temps a changé.
(C) La narratrice a décidé de partir.
(D) La narratrice a trouvé un amant.

Antoine Lemurier, qui avait manqué mourir, sortit
heureusement de maladie, reprit son service au bureau,
*Ligne* et, tant bien que mal, pansa ses plaies d'argent. Durant
cette épreuve, les voisins s'étaient réjouis en pensant que
5 le mari allait crever, le mobilier être vendu, la femme
à la rue. Tous étaient d'ailleurs d'excellentes gens, des
cœurs d'or, comme tout le monde, et n'en voulaient
nullement au ménage Lemurier, mais voyant se jouer
auprès d'eux une sombre tragédie avec rebonds, péripéties,
10 beuglements de proprio, huissier et fièvre montante, ils
vivaient anxieusement dans l'attente d'un dénouement qui
fût digne de la pièce.
(Marcel Aymé, *Les Sabines*, Folio)

21. On comprend qu'Antoine Lemurier

    (A) est mort
    (B) a raté le train
    (C) a quitté son bureau
    (D) a failli succomber à une maladie

22. Qu'est-ce que les voisins pensaient de la maladie de
    Lemurier?

    (A) Ils attendaient une fin intéressante à la tragédie.
    (B) Ils étaient tristes.
    (C) Ils étaient fâchés contre Lemurier.
    (D) Ils tombaient malades.

23. Selon les voisins, qu'est-ce qui serait "un
    dénouement . . . digne" de la situation?

    (A) M. Lemurier perd son travail.
    (B) M. Lemurier récupère complètement.
    (C) Mme Lemurier est sans abri.
    (D) Mme Lemurier vend la maison.

# Summary

For Part D, Reading Comprehension, practice is the best way to improve your score. Make sure you do the following:

- Memorize the instructions to save time on test day.

- Read the questions first so you know what to look for in the passage.

- Read and eliminate wrong answer choices.

- Do not get stuck on difficult passages or questions. Move on and come back later if you have the time.

# Chapter 7
# French Listening

The SAT French Subject Test with Listening evaluates your reading and listening skills of spoken French. It is about one hour long: 20 minutes for listening and 40 minutes for reading questions.

The test is only administered in November at designated test centers. You will need to fill out a special registration form and find the testing center nearest to you. On test day, you must take an appropriate CD player with earphones.

In this chapter, we explore the overall structure and describe each part of the listening test.

## OVERALL STRUCTURE OF THE LISTENING TEST

The SAT French Subject Test with Listening consists of **40 minutes of reading (written questions)** and **20 minutes of listening (oral questions)**, with 85 to 90 questions in all. This means that about two-thirds of the SAT French Subject Test with Listening consists of questions we've already discussed. You will have 40 minutes to work on those. There are, however, fewer of each type.

- Part A—Vocabulary Completions: 12–16 questions
- Part B—Grammar Blanks: 12–16 questions
- Part C—Paragraph Blanks: 15–17 questions
- Part D—Reading Comprehension: 20–25 questions

In addition to those regular questions, you will have 20 minutes to work on the listening part of the test. There will be three parts with a total of about 40 questions covering pictures (8–12 questions), short dialogues (6-12 questions), and long dialogues (10-15 questions).

- Listening—Part A: Pictures
- Listening—Part B: Short Dialogues
- Listening—Part C: Longer Dialogues

Samples of each type of question are available on the College Board's website, www.collegeboard.com.

## Should You Sign Up for the French Subject Test with Listening?

The results of your test will give colleges a more complete picture of your French language proficiency. Your aim should be to give them the best picture of your abilities for the purpose of class placement.

You do not have to speak French on either of the SAT French Subject Tests. Therefore, do not feel anxious about the listening portion of the test. Many students tend to do better on this section than they do on the written portion. There are fewer grammar and reading questions, which will benefit students who are better at spoken French than at grammar or reading comprehension. To prepare for the listening test you may want to visit www.laguinguette.com. You'll also find it helpful to watch and listen to French TV news and as many French movies as you can get your hands on.

# LISTENING—PART A: PICTURES

The first part of the Listening Test consists of choosing which spoken phrase best matches the provided picture. Each sentence will be designated (A), (B), (C), or (D).

> **Directions:** For each item in this part, you will hear four sentences designated (A), (B), (C), and (D). They will not be printed in your test booklet. As you listen, look at the picture in your test booklet and select the choice that best reflects what you see in the picture or what someone in the picture might say. Then fill in the corresponding oval on the answer sheet. You will hear the choices only once. Now look at the following example.

Look at the picture before the answer choices are played. Get a general idea of what is going on.

## Make a Decision as You Hear Each Choice

As each answer choice is read to you, decide if that choice is at all appropriate. If it is not, cross out that choice on your answer sheet. You may not be allowed to write in your book. If the choice is good or possible, make a small mark inside the bubble. Probably only one will make any sense. If not, guess. **Don't wait to hear all the choices before deciding about each of them.** Decide "yes" or "no" as you go, for you will hear each choice only one time, so you must think quickly. Erase all stray marks once you select an answer.

## LISTENING—PART B: SHORT DIALOGUES

On this section you will hear either a dialogue between two people, or a monologue. It will be followed by three answer choices labeled (A), (B), or (C). The answer choices will be heard only once. Again, listen closely because nothing is repeated.

## Make a Decision as You Hear Each Choice

As you hear each answer choice, decide if it is appropriate or not. Eliminate it or keep it on your answer sheet. Once you've selected an answer, erase all stray marks. Do not mark (D) or (E) as choices.

## LISTENING—PART C: LONG PASSAGES

This section consists of longer monologues or dialogues that will be heard only once. In this section, the questions and the four answer choices will be in the test booklet.

**Hear Ye, Hear Ye**
On Part C of the listening part of the test, answer the questions as you hear the information being presented. Don't wait to hear the whole thing!

## Forewarned, Forearmed

The great thing about this question type in Part C is that the questions and answer choices are printed in your booklet. As the instructions are being read (familiarize yourself with them now so that you don't waste time on test day) and before the passage is read, read the questions and their answers to get a sense of the topic.

As in reading comprehension, the questions are in chronological order. Don't wait for the entire passage to be read before answering the questions. (It would be hard for even a native speaker to remember all those details for very long.) As the passage is being read, look at each question and mark the correct answer as soon as you hear it. The questions will either ask you to repeat specific details or paraphrase them. You are not required to interpret or infer.

# Summary

Practice is the number one way to improve your score on the SAT French Listening Test. In order to get your best score, make sure you do the following:

- Memorize the instructions to save time on test day.

- Bring the required CD player and fresh batteries.

- Go to the test rested and well fed.

- Follow the pace of the recording.

- Make your decision as you hear the choices because you won't remember them if you wait.

- If there is a picture, look at all the details.

- On the Long Passages section, do not wait for the entire passage to be read. Answer as soon as you figure out the right choice.

# Part III
# Drill Answers
# and Explanations

# CHAPTER 3 DRILL ANSWERS AND EXPLANATIONS

## Drill 1

| | |
|---|---|
| *une usine* | a factory |
| *la honte* | the shame |
| *l'œuvre* | the work |
| *en vouloir à* | to be angry at, to have a grudge against |
| *mou* | soft, limp, looseness |
| *taquiner* | to tease |
| *la foule* | the crowd |
| *ramasser* | to gather, to pick up |
| *soutenir* | to support, to sustain |
| *repasser* | to come back, to cross again, to iron |
| *se méfier de* | to distrust, to be suspicious |
| *se débarrasser de* | to get rid of |

## Drill 2

| | |
|---|---|
| *évaluer* | to evaluate |
| *sacré* | sacred |
| *retarder* | to delay, to slow down |
| *fréquenter* | to go somewhere frequently, to see someone on a regular basis |
| *nombre* | number |
| *assurer* | to assure |
| *raison* | reason |
| *plante* | plant |
| *attraper* | to catch, to trap |
| *servir* | to serve |
| *content* | content or happy |
| *accord* | accord or harmony |
| *cru* | crude or raw |

## Drill 3

| Question | Answer | Explanation |
|---|---|---|
| 1.  xxxxx xxxxxxxx légumes xxxx xxxxx . . . vegetables | B | (A) *cheminée*<br>chimney<br>(B) *jardin*<br>**garden**<br>(C) *gazon*<br>lawn<br>(D) *quartier*<br>quarter or neighborhood |
| 2.  xxxx xxxxxxx x *tombée* xxx xxxx . . . fallen | C | (A) *envolée*<br>taken flight<br>(B) *échappée*<br>escaped<br>(C) *cassée*<br>**broken**<br>(D) *attrapée*<br>caught |

| Question | Answer | Explanation |
|---|---|---|
| 3. xx x xxx xxxxx *chaises* xxxx . . . xxxx xx xxxxx. chairs | B | (A) *assommer* <br> to knock out <br> **(B) *s'asseoir*** <br> **to sit down** <br> (C) *assurer* <br> to assure <br> (D) *associer* <br> to associate |
| 4. xxx xxxx *ne se sent pas bien* xxxxx xxx . . . doesn't feel well | A | **(A) *une fièvre*** <br> **a fever** <br> (B) *une armoire* <br> a wardrobe <br> (C) *un verger* <br> an orchard <br> (D) *une annonce* <br> an announcement |
| 5. xxxxx xxxx xxxxxxxxx xxxxx *mangé* xxx xxx . . . eaten | C | (A) *soutenir* <br> to support <br> (B) *emporter* <br> to take or carry away <br> **(C) *avaler*** <br> **to swallow** <br> (D) *évaluer* <br> to evaluate |

# Comprehensive Drill

## Part A

| Question | | Answer | Key Word or Phrase | Fill In |
|---|---|---|---|---|
| 1 | It's cold outside. Are all the . . . closed? | C | *fait froid* | windows |
| 2 | Don't make any noise; the children are . . . | B | *bruit, enfants* | asleep |
| 3 | Are these flowers from your . . . ? | C | *fleurs* | garden |
| 4 | This coat lacks . . . where I can put my wallet. | C | *manteau, porte-monnaie* | pockets |
| 5 | Jeanne woke up . . . in order to see the sunrise. | D | *lever du soleil* | early |
| 6 | The train left the . . . at noon. | D | *train* | station |
| 7 | For Sunday's meal, we eat a . . . with potatoes. | A | *repas* | a roast |
| 8 | The tarts that are sold in this . . . are delicious. | A | *tartes* | pastry shop |
| 9 | You can wash yourself now. The bathroom is . . . | B | *salle de bains* | open, empty |
| 10 | My . . . for class is to translate a poem of Rimbaud's. | D | *classe* | homework, assignment |
| 11 | The noise in a club can be so loud that it hurts one's . . . | A | *bruit* | ears |
| 12 | The moon is so . . . that I cannot imagine that man has gone there. | C | *lune* | far away |
| 13 | It's not necessary to take out the garbage; Jean did it . . . | C | *l'a . . . fait* | already |
| 14 | We are spending Christmas with my grandparents this . . . | C | *Noël* | winter |
| 15 | You've already done your homework? That . . . | D | *déjà* | surprises me, pleases me |

| Question | | Answer | Key Word or Phrase | Fill In |
|---|---|---|---|---|
| 16 | Aren't you . . . of doing that stupid thing? | D | *bêtise* | ashamed, embarrassed |
| 17 | This fabric is . . . like the skin of a baby. | C | *peau d'un bébé* | soft |
| 18 | The fox . . . the hunters. | C | *renard, chasseurs* | escaped from |
| 19 | The film starts at exactly 8 o'clock; be . . . | A | *commence* | on time, early |
| 20 | There are too many people here; I prefer cafés that are less . . . | D | *trop de monde* | crowded |
| 21 | There is not enough evidence . . . this man. | D | *pas assez de preuves* | to convict, charge, indict |
| 22 | My brother is . . . ; he never wants to help me clean the kitchen. | B | *il ne veut jamais m'aider* | lazy, selfish |
| 23 | The vase that I dropped . . . | D | *laissé tomber* | broke, shattered |
| 24 | You can find your grandmother's wedding dress if you look in . . . | B | *la robe de mariée de votre grand-mère* | the attic |
| 25 | She got rid of her . . . clothing. | C | *s'est débarrassée* | unwanted, messed up |
| 26 | Diane cut her . . . so she would be more fashionable. | C | *s'est coupé* | hair |
| 27 | To establish the validity of his theory, the scientist conducted . . . | B | *établir la validité* | an experiment, study |

# CHAPTER 5 DRILL ANSWERS AND EXPLANATIONS

## Drill 1: Pronoun Questions

| Question | | Answer | Explanation |
|---|---|---|---|
| 1 | ------- *est arrivé à Paul hier?*<br>What happened to Paul yesterday? | D | (A) *Quel*<br>*Quel* means "which" and is used to modify a noun (*Quelle voiture est la vôtre?*). We need something that means "what."<br>(B) *Quoi*<br>In questions, *quoi* is used only with a preposition (*À quoi sert cet exercice?*).<br>(C) *Qu'*<br>*Qu'* is a shortened form of *que*. Since the "what" of the question is the subject (what happened), it cannot be *que*.<br>(D) **Qu'est-ce qui is correct. You cannot use *qui* alone because that would mean "who happened to Paul yesterday?" And you need *qui* here because it is directly followed by a verb.** |
| 2 | *C'est -------.*<br>It is he. | C | With *c'est* or *ce sont* you use either a noun or a stressed pronoun.<br>(A) *eux*<br>*Eux* is a stressed pronoun, which is proper, but since it is plural, the correct sentence would be *Ce sont eux*.<br>(B) *il*<br>*Il* is a subject pronoun. No good here.<br>(C) *lui*<br>**Lui can be a singular stressed pronoun. This is the correct answer.**<br>(D) *le*<br>*Le* is a direct object pronoun. Cancel it. |

| Question | | Answer | Explanation |
|---|---|---|---|
| 3 | *C'est grâce à ------- que nous avons pu venir.*<br>It is thanks to them that we could come. | A | Because the pronoun is being used with a preposition (but not as an indirect object), we want a stressed pronoun.<br>(A) *eux*<br>**Eux is a stressed pronoun, so this is the correct choice.**<br>(B) *les*<br>*Les* is the direct object pronoun.<br>(C) *leur*<br>*Leur* is the indirect object pronoun.<br>(D) *ils*<br>*Ils* is the subject pronoun. |
| 4 | *La chose la plus difficile est de ------- réveiller le matin.*<br>The most difficult thing is to wake him up in the morning. | C | The verb in this sentence is *réveiller*, a verb that takes a direct object. The correct answer must serve as a direct object pronoun.<br>(A) *lui*<br>*Lui* can be an indirect object pronoun or a stressed pronoun.<br>(B) *il*<br>*Il* is the subject pronoun.<br>(C) *le*<br>**Le is the direct object pronoun, so this is the correct answer.**<br>(D) *moi*<br>*Moi* is the stressed pronoun. |

| Question | | Answer | Explanation |
|---|---|---|---|
| 5 | ------- *a sorti la poubelle.*<br>No one took out the garbage. | B | (A) *Il n'*<br>This choice does not work because the sentence lacks the *pas* that must be used with *ne* (*n'*) to make a negative.<br>(B) *Personne n'*<br>This is the correct answer. *Personne* must be used with *ne* and does not need the *pas*.<br>(C) *Aucun*<br>Like *personne*, *aucun* must be used with *ne*.<br>(D) *Qui*<br>*Qui* can begin the sentence in a question, but not in a statement. |

## Drill 2: Verb Questions

| Question | | Answer | Explanation |
|---|---|---|---|
| 1 | *Si -------, je préparerais le dîner.*<br>If I had time, I would make dinner. | C | Since the conditional tense is used in the portion of the sentence following the blank, the verb that precedes it must be in the **imperfect**. Only choice (C) has a verb in the imperfect.<br>(A) *vous en avez envie*—present<br>(B) *on me le demande*—present<br>(C) *j'avais le temps*—**imperfect**<br>(D) *tu seras d'accord*—future |
| 2 | *Paul regrette que nous ------- pas réussi.*<br>Paul regrets that we have not succeeded. | C | What mode is used with verbs like *regretter que*? The subjunctive. Only choice (C) has the subjunctive.<br>(A) *n'avons*—present<br>(B) *n'avions*—imperfect<br>(C) *n'ayons*—**subjunctive (present)**<br>(D) *n'aurons*—future |

| Question | | Answer | Explanation |
|---|---|---|---|
| 3 | ------ *une lettre quand on a sonné à la porte.* <br> I was writing a letter when the doorbell rang. | D | The use of the *passé composé* indicates that the sentence takes place in the past, so you can eliminate (A), (B), and (C). The answer is (D). The use of the imperfect indicates that the action of letter writing was ongoing when the doorbell rang. <br> (A) *J'écris*—present <br> (B) *J'écrirais*—conditional <br> (C) *J'écrive*—subjunctive (present) <br> **(D) *J'écrivais*—imperfect** |
| 4 | *Elle n'a jamais oublié ce que nous ------- au moment de son départ.* <br> She never forgot what we said at the moment of her departure. | C | Does the expression *ce que* take the subjunctive? No. Eliminate (B). The use of the *passé composé* in the first part of the sentence indicates that the sentence takes place in the past and the verb does not need to be in the subjective or conditional mood. Eliminate (A) and (D). The correct answer is (C). <br> (A) *disons*—present <br> (B) *ayons dit*—past of the subjunctive <br> **(C) *avons dit*—*passé composé*** <br> (D) *aurions dit*—past of the conditional |
| 5 | *Est-ce que vous ------- contents si je n'avais pas accepté l'invitation?* <br> Would you have been happy if I had not accepted the invitation? | D | Since a form of the imperfect is being used with *si*, the other verb must be in the conditional. Choice (D) is the only verb in the conditional. Since one part of the sentence has the past form of the imperfect (the *plus-que-parfait*), it makes sense that the conditional verb would also be in a past form. <br> (A) *êtes*—present <br> (B) *soyez*—subjunctive <br> (C) *étiez*—imperfect <br> **(D) *auriez été*—past of the conditional** |
| 6 | *Nous doutons ------- leur rendre visite chez eux.* <br> We doubt that he has time to visit them. | A | Does the verb *douter que* take the subjunctive? Yes, so (B), (C), and (D) must be wrong. Choice (A) is the correct answer because the subjunctive is used. <br> **(A) *qu'il ait le temps de*—subjunctive** <br> (B) *qu'il voudrait*—conditional <br> (C) *qu'il peut*—present <br> (D) *qu'elle avait envie de*—imperfect |

| Question | Answer | Explanation |
|---|---|---|
| 7 | ------- , *elle est partie pour le long trajet chez elle.*<br>Having said goodbye, she left for the long journey home. | C | We need a verb form that shows when she said goodbye (the verb is in all the answer choices). We can eliminate (B), since it is the infinitive and the sentence is in the past. To show that she said goodbye either before or as she left, we need either the perfect or the present participle. The only participle here is (C), the perfect participle, "having said goodbye." This is our answer. The other choices, (A) and (D), cannot be used by themselves in a phrase.<br>(A) *Disait au revoir*—imperfect<br>(B) *Dire au revoir*—infinitive<br>(C) **Ayant dit au revoir—perfect participle**<br>(D) *Avoir dit au revoir*—past infinitive |
| 8 | *Tu pourras regarder la télé une fois que tu* --------- *ton travail.*<br>You will be allowed to watch TV once you have finished your homework. | C | Does the conjunction *une fois que* take the subjunctive? No. Eliminate (D). We need a verb form that shows that your homework must be finished in the future before you may watch TV. Choice (B) is the imperfect so it does not work. Choice (A) is the past form of the conditional, so it does not work either. The correct answer is (C), futur antérieur, future perfect tense.<br>(A) aurais fini—past conditional<br>(B) finissais—imperfect<br>(C) **auras fini—future perfect**<br>(D) finisses—subjunctive |

# Drill 3: Preposition Questions

| Question | Answer | Explanation |
|---|---|---|
| 1 *Marie ------- les résultats de ses examens.* Marie is waiting for the results of her exams. | B | (A) *pense* <br> Penser requires the preposition *à* or *de*. <br> **(B) *attend*** <br> ***Attendre* requires no preposition. This is the correct answer.** <br> (C) *compte* <br> *Compter* requires the preposition *sur*. Without a preposition, it means "to count" and makes no sense here. <br> (D) *a envie* <br> *Avoir envie* requires the preposition *de*. |
| 2 *Je ------- de leur écrire.* I am compelled to write them. | A | **(A) *suis obligé*** <br> **This is the correct answer. *Être obligé* requires the preposition *de*.** <br> (B) *espère* <br> *Espérer* takes no preposition in French. <br> (C) *veux* <br> *Vouloir* takes no preposition. It cannot be used with *de*. <br> (D) *réfléchis* <br> *Réfléchir* takes the preposition *à*. It cannot be used with *de*. |
| 3 *Je n'ai jamais eu l'occasion ------- voir ce film.* I have never had the opportunity to see this film. | C | The expression *avoir l'occasion* takes the preposition *de*. **(C) is the correct answer.** |

| Question | | Answer | Explanation |
|---|---|---|---|
| 4 | ------- *le concert, elles bavardaient sans cesse.*<br>During the concert, they chattered end-lessly. | A | (A) *Pendant*<br>***Pendant* means "during." This is the correct answer.**<br>(B) *Dans*<br>*Dans* means "in." You cannot say *dans le concert.*<br>(C) *Avec*<br>*Avec* means "with." You might find a context in which *avec* works with *le concert*, but in this context, it does not.<br>(D) *En*<br>There might be a context in which *en concert* is acceptable, but *en le concert* is never correct. |
| 5 | *Je la vois souvent à -------.*<br>I see her often at the bakery. | C | (A) *France*<br>The correct expression would be *en France.*<br>(B) *ville*<br>You can say either *à la ville* or *en ville.*<br>**(C) *la boulangerie***<br>**This is the correct answer. You can say *à la boulangerie.***<br>(D) *loin*<br>*Loin* is never used with *à.* |
| 6 | *Elle n'a pas réfléchi ------- de refuser l'offre.*<br>She did not think before refusing the offer. | B | (A) ---<br>*Réfléchir* must be used with a preposition.<br>**(B) *avant***<br>**This is the correct answer.**<br>(C) *après*<br>You cannot say *après de. Après* is used with the infinitive (e.g., *après avoir réfléchi*).<br>(D) *à*<br>You cannot have these two prepositions, *à* and *de*, following each other. |

# Comprehensive Drill

## Part B

| Question | Category | Answer | Explanation |
|---|---|---|---|
| 1 | Odds and Ends | A | **(A)** *quelque chose* is correct <br> (B) *rien* must be used with *ne*—*n'a rien* <br> (C) *plusieurs* must modify a noun <br> (D) *quelque* must modify a noun |
| 2 | Prepositions | C | (A) *rejeter* cannot be followed by a verb <br> (B) *aimer* takes the infinitive <br> **(C)** *être obligé* takes *de*, so it is correct <br> (D) *avoir voulu* takes the infinitive |
| 3 | Odds and Ends | B | (A) plural <br> **(B)** *amie* is feminine, but it's correct because *amie* begins with a vowel <br> (C) feminine <br> (D) plural |
| 4 | Odds and Ends | A | **(A)** *avant de partir* works with the future tense <br> (B) *tout à l'heure* is okay, but not with *à* <br> (C) *hier* does not work with the future <br> (D) *jamais* must be used with *ne* |
| 5 | Pronouns | D | (A) *personne* requires *ne* <br> (B) subject pronoun <br> (C) indirect object <br> **(D)** stressed pronoun is correct with *c'est* |
| 6 | Prepositions | A | **(A)** *préférer* takes the infinitive—correct <br> (B) *rêver* takes *de* and then the infinitive <br> (C) *plaire* takes no direct object <br> (D) *insister* takes *pour* and the infinitive |
| 7 | Pronouns | D | (A) subject or stressed pronoun <br> (B) stressed pronoun <br> (C) reflexive, but wrong person <br> **(D)** *demander quelque chose à quelqu'un*—indirect object is correct |

| Question | Category | Answer | Explanation |
|---|---|---|---|
| 8 | Pronouns | C | (A) indirect object pronoun<br>(B) subject pronoun<br>**(C) stressed pronoun is correct with *avec***<br>(D) direct object pronoun |
| 9 | Pronouns | B | (A) plural<br>**(B) singular and feminine possessive pronoun—correct**<br>(C) *aucun* requires *ne*<br>(D) possessive adjective |
| 10 | Prepositions | A | **(A) *Russie* is feminine—correct with *en***<br>(B) *États-Unis* is plural (*aux*)<br>(C) New York takes *à*<br>(D) Canada is masculine (*au*) |
| 11 | Odds and Ends | C | (A) adverb<br>(B) adverb<br>**(C) adjective—correct**<br>(D) preposition |
| 12 | Verbs | B | (A) *savoir que* doesn't take the subjunctive<br>**(B) *regretter que* takes the subjunctive—correct**<br>(C) *oublier que* doesn't take the subjunctive<br>(D) nothing hypothetical, so no subjunctive |
| 13 | Pronouns/Prepositions | A | **(A) *parler* takes *de*—therefore *dont* is correct**<br>(B) *quoi* is used with things<br>(C) *parler* cannot work with *sauf*<br>(D) *avant que* is a conjunction, not a pronoun |
| 14 | Pronouns | C | (A) *quelle* is feminine<br>(B) *qu'est-ce qui* is used to refer to things<br>**(C) *où* means "where"—correct**<br>(D) *quoi* is used with things |
| 15 | Pronouns | D | (A) *quel* must modify something<br>(B) *y* refers to place or location<br>(C) *dont* cannot be used to begin a question<br>**(D) *avoir envie* takes *de*—correct** |

| Question | Category | Answer | Explanation |
|----------|----------|--------|-------------|
| 16 | Prepositions | C | (A) *aller* does not take *de* <br> (B) *espérer* takes either the infinitive or *que* <br> (C) *essayer* takes *de*—correct <br> (D) *pouvoir* does not take *de* |
| 17 | Verbs | C | (A) *sans doute* means "probably" <br> (B) certain, so no subjunctive <br> (C) *Je crains* means "I fear." This expression takes the subjunctive—correct <br> (D) no doubt or uncertainty, so no subjunctive |
| 18 | Prepositions | C | (A) in order to <br> (B) when <br> (C) in spite of—correct <br> (D) unless |
| 19 | Verbs | A | (A) imperfect followed by conditional—correct <br> (B) present, so following clause can't be conditional <br> (C) future cannot follow *si* <br> (D) past imperfect would take past conditional |
| 20 | Verbs | D | (A) *passé composé* <br> (B) *passé composé* <br> (C) *passé composé* <br> (D) subjunctive is used with superlatives—correct |

## Part C

| Question | Category | Answer | Explanation |
|----------|----------|--------|-------------|
| 21 | Verbs | D | (A) imperfect <br> (B) past imperfect <br> (C) present <br> (D) past conditional follows a clause with *si* and the past imperfect—correct |
| 22 | Pronouns | B | (A) subject or stressed pronoun <br> (B) indirect object—correct <br> (C) stressed pronoun and masculine <br> (D) direct object and singular |

| Question | Category | Answer | Explanation |
|----------|----------|--------|-------------|
| 23 | Pronouns | A | (A) **stressed pronoun with *chez*—correct** <br> (B) subject <br> (C) indirect object <br> (D) subject and masculine |
| 24 | Vocabulary | A | (A) **no one—correct** <br> (B) a person <br> (C) nothing <br> (D) *nulle* is an adjective |
| 25 | Vocabulary | A | (A) **Finally—correct** <br> (B) *Terminé* is not an adverb, but a past participle <br> (C) Now <br> (D) In order to |
| 26 | Pronouns | B | (A) *arriver de* makes no sense in this context <br> (B) ***y* indicates place: in this case, the café—correct** <br> (C) *le* is a direct object pronoun <br> (D) *arriver* cannot be reflexive |
| 27 | Verbs | D | (A) no agreement or masculine singular <br> (B) feminine singular <br> (C) masculine plural <br> (D) **feminine plural: requires agreement because direct object precedes verb—correct** |
| 28 | Prepositions | B | (A) *cinéma* is masculine <br> (B) ***au* is correct because *cinéma* is masculine** <br> (C) *entrer par* doesn't make sense in this context and *cinéma* is masculine <br> (D) *entrer par* doesn't make sense in this context |
| 29 | Prepositions | C | (A) you cannot use *avant* and a verb without a preposition <br> (B) *avant à* does not exist <br> (C) **the correct expression is *avant de*** <br> (D) *avant que* would have to be followed by a clause using the subjunctive |
| 30 | Verbs | A | (A) **no agreement required—correct** <br> (B) feminine <br> (C) masculine plural <br> (D) feminine plural |

| Question | Category | Answer | Explanation |
|---|---|---|---|
| 31 | Prepositions | D | (A) needs a preposition to make sense<br>(B) *à demander* makes no sense<br>(C) *de demander* makes no sense<br>**(D) *pour demander*: to ask—correct** |
| 32 | Conjunctions | A | **(A) *si*—correct**<br>(B) when<br>(C) which<br>(D) who |
| 33 | Vocabulary | C | (A) *en temps* does not exist; *à temps* (on time) would be correct<br>(B) every hour<br>**(C) on time—correct**<br>(D) from time to time |

# CHAPTER 6 DRILL ANSWERS AND EXPLANATIONS

## Comprehensive Drill

### Part D

| Question | | Answer | Explanation |
|---|---|---|---|
| 1 | Etienne lacked the energy to | B | (A) "sleep": familiar word—wrong context<br>**(B) "undress": see phrase *tout vêtu* (fully dressed)**<br>(C) "eat"<br>(D) "put on his clothes" |
| 2 | According to the passage, why is Etienne tired? | D | (A) "He ate too much." familiar words—wrong context<br>(B) "He did not sleep at all in two days." Too extreme; he did get some sleep.<br>(C) "He went to sleep at four in the morning." familiar words—wrong context<br>**(D) "He has slept only for a few hours in 48 hours": see *En deux jours, il n'avait pas dormi quatre heures*.** |

| Question | | Answer | Explanation |
|---|---|---|---|
| 3 | At what time of day did he get up? | C | (A) "early in the morning" <br> (B) "noon" <br> **(C) "early in the evening": see *au crépuscule, avant de . . . se coucher pour la nuit*** <br> (D) "midnight" |
| 4 | How does he react at the moment he wakes up? | A | **(A) "He doesn't remember where he is": see *sans reconnaître le lieu où il se trouvait*** <br> (B) "He can't find his clothes." <br> (C) "He feels that he is late." <br> (D) "He is hungry." |
| 5 | What did he want to do before eating dinner? | B | (A) "breathe" <br> **(B) "go for a walk": see *prendre l'air*** <br> (C) "wake up": familiar words—wrong context <br> (D) "run" |
| 6 | When did Morissot leave to reach the island? | C | (A) "after sunset" <br> (B) "at sunset" <br> **(C) "at sunrise": see *dès l'aurore*** <br> (D) "in the afternoon" |
| 7 | How did he reach the island? | D | (A) "by bus and on foot" <br> (B) "by boat" <br> (C) "by car and on foot" <br> **(D) "by train and on foot": see *chemin de fer* (railway), *à pied*** |
| 8 | At what point did he start fishing? | A | **(A) "at almost the moment he arrived": see *à peine arrivé*** <br> (B) "at the moment he started to dream" <br> (C) "at nightfall" <br> (D) "when his friend arrived" |
| 9 | What is located on Notre-Dame-de-Lorette Street? | C | (A) "the island": makes no sense <br> (B) "the place the two friends would meet" <br> **(C) "Mr. Savage's shop": see *mercier* (dealer in sewing wares)** <br> (D) "the train station" |
| 10 | The parents of Guillaume | D | (A) "advise him never to go to the movies" <br> (B) "don't concern themselves with what he does" <br> (C) "don't like the movies" <br> **(D) "give their opinion about the films he chooses": see *je leur demande ce qu'ils en pensent*** |

| Question | | Answer | Explanation |
|---|---|---|---|
| 11 | To Gilles's question, Claire replies | C | (A) "that she never goes to the movies"<br>(B) "that she goes to the movies if her parents agree"<br>**(C) "that she goes to the movies without telling her parents": see _en cachette_ (secretly)**<br>(D) "that she goes to the movies often" |
| 12 | What reason does Guillaume give for not lying to his parents? | B | (A) "His parents let him do anything.": familiar words—wrong context<br>**(B) "His parents let him decide what to do.": see _Je crois que je me sens libre_**<br>(C) "It is better not to do it."<br>(D) "His parents don't like the movies." |
| 13 | The author reacts to the change in Boulevard St. Michel and Place Saint-André-des-Arts with | B | (A) "impatience"<br>**(B) "regret"**<br>(C) "indifference"<br>(D) "pleasure": makes no sense |
| 14 | What does one find near Luxembourg? | D | (A) "small, anonymous restaurants": familiar words—wrong context<br>(B) "pleasant cafés": familiar words—wrong context<br>(C) "pretentious bookstores"<br>**(D) "American establishments": _McDonald's_** |
| 15 | According to the passage, "Gibert" is | C | (A) "a film"<br>(B) "a café"<br>**(C) "a bookstore": see _cinémas et librairies semblent résister_**<br>(D) "a museum" |
| 16 | What do young people do instead of going to Boulevard St. Michel? | C | (A) "They go to Place Saint-André-des-Arts."<br>(B) "They are in a rush to see American films."<br>**(C) "They look for cool bars in another area.": see _autour du Panthéon_**<br>(D) "They resist going to bookstores." |
| 17 | The narrator lets it be understood that she | D | (A) "worked a lot"<br>(B) "was an invalid"<br>(C) "had many worries"<br>**(D) "married her father's friend": see _Un vieil ami de mon père m'a demandé ma main._** |

| Question | | Answer | Explanation |
|---|---|---|---|
| 18 | The brother of the narrator | B | (A) "lived with her for six years": familiar words—wrong context<br>**(B) "was younger than she":** *cadet*<br>(C) "was a soldier"<br>(D) "didn't like her husband" |
| 19 | The passage gives us the impression | A | **(A) "that she wanted to defend her actions": see** *Qu'auriez-vous fait à ma place?*<br>(B) "that she missed her husband"<br>(C) "that her brother was cured"<br>(D) "that she liked good weather": misunderstanding, as *sans un nuage* is not literal |
| 20 | After six years, what happened? | D | (A) "The husband of the narrator left."<br>(B) "The good weather changed.": *sans un nuage* is not literal<br>(C) "The narrator decided to leave."<br>**(D) "The narrator found a lover.": see** *j'ai rencontré celui que je devais aimer.* |
| 21 | It is understood that Antoine Lemurier | D | (A) "is dead"<br>(B) "missed the train"<br>(C) "left his work"<br>**(D) "nearly succumbed to an illness": see** *avait manqué mourir* (almost died) |
| 22 | What did the neighbors think of Lemurier's illness? | A | **(A) "They expected an interesting end to the tragedy.": see** *ils vivaient anxieusement dans l'attente d'un dénouement qui fût digne de la pièce*<br>(B) "They were sad."<br>(C) "They were angry with Lemurier."<br>(D) "They fell ill." |
| 23 | According to the neighbors, what would have been a fitting end to the situation? | C | (A) "Mr. Lemurier loses his job."<br>(B) "Mr. Lemurier completely recovers."<br>**(C) "Mrs. Lemurier is without shelter.": see** *la femme à la rue*<br>(D) "Mrs. Lemurier sells the house.": close, but the phrase is *le mobilier être vendu* |

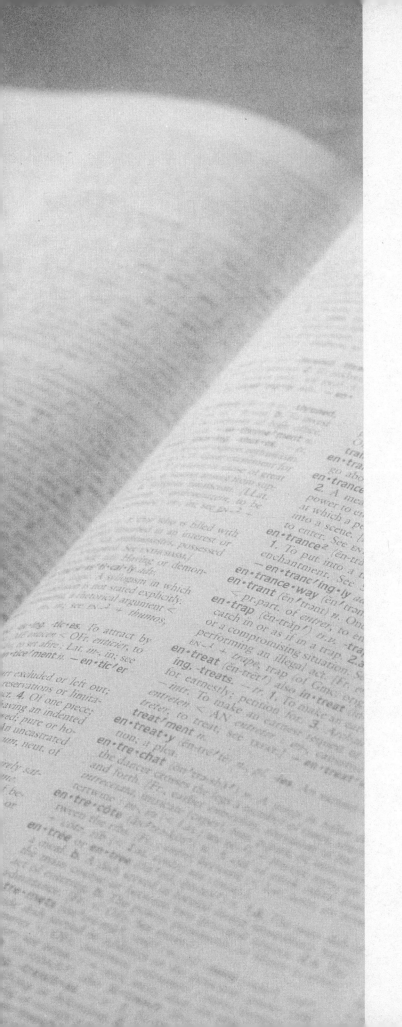

# Part IV
# Practice Tests

# Chapter 8
# Practice Test 1

# FRENCH SUBJECT TEST 1

## SECTION 1

Your responses to the SAT French questions must be filled in on Section 1 of your answer sheet (at the back of the book). Marks on any other section will not be counted toward your score.

When your supervisor gives the signal, turn the page and begin the SAT French Subject Test.

# FRENCH SUBJECT TEST 1

PLEASE NOTE THAT YOUR ANSWER SHEET HAS FIVE ANSWER POSITIONS, MARKED A, B, C, D, E, WHILE THE QUESTIONS THROUGHOUT THIS TEST CONTAIN ONLY FOUR CHOICES. BE SURE <u>NOT</u> TO MAKE ANY MARKS IN COLUMN E.

## Part A

**Directions:** This part consists of a number of incomplete statements, each having four suggested completions. Select the most appropriate completion and fill in the corresponding oval on the answer sheet.

1. Les documents dont j'ai besoin pour mon travail sont toujours dans ma . . . au bureau.

   (A) douche
   (B) mallette
   (C) fourneau
   (D) pot à fleur

2. Il fait beau dehors; veux-tu te . . . après le dîner?

   (A) laver
   (B) demander
   (C) lever
   (D) promener

3. Le soldat attendait avec impatience la fin de . . .

   (A) la route
   (B) la gare
   (C) la guerre
   (D) l'immeuble

4. Il n'est pas permis d'amener votre chien . . . le café; veuillez le laisser à l'extérieur.

   (A) dans
   (B) avec
   (C) en dehors de
   (D) après

5. Paul a besoin d' . . . pour soutenir son pantalon.

   (A) un bras
   (B) une poche
   (C) une jambe
   (D) une ceinture

6. Pour son anniversaire, le garçon a reçu plusieurs . . .

   (A) jours
   (B) talents
   (C) jardins
   (D) cadeaux

7. Le tailleur nous a fait de nouveaux . . .

   (A) pneus
   (B) pains
   (C) vêtements
   (D) ameublement

8. Le . . . de mon immeuble est 564.

   (A) nombre
   (B) guide
   (C) numéro
   (D) nom

**GO ON TO THE NEXT PAGE**

9. Il y a douze . . . dans un an.

   (A) mois
   (B) jours
   (C) heures
   (D) saisons

10. La route est fermée; nous ne pouvons pas . . . n'importe où.

    (A) conduire
    (B) acheter
    (C) jouer
    (D) sauter

11. Quand je porte mes souliers préférés, je n'ai jamais mal aux . . .

    (A) coudes
    (B) pieds
    (C) lèvres
    (D) oreilles

12. Je suis d'accord avec lui; je pense qu'il a . . .

    (A) tort
    (B) raison
    (C) mal
    (D) nécessité

13. Le magasin n'est pas . . . de mon bureau, alors je peux y aller à pied en cinq minutes.

    (A) en haut
    (B) tout près
    (C) sur
    (D) loin

14. Le héros a . . . une fille qui était en train de se noyer.

    (A) sauvé
    (B) nagé
    (C) remercié
    (D) traîné

15. L'été, il faut porter des . . . de soleil pour se protéger les yeux.

    (A) spectacles
    (B) cheveux
    (C) lunettes
    (D) rayons

16. Il est important de . . . des questions à votre enseignant si vous ne comprenez pas votre manuel.

    (A) enseigner
    (B) poser
    (C) être ennuyé avec
    (D) exiger

**GO ON TO THE NEXT PAGE**

17. Ce n'est pas gentil de . . . tes amis.

   (A) lire
   (B) remplir
   (C) taquiner
   (D) tolérer

18. Le bruit constant m'. . .

   (A) énerve
   (B) enseigne
   (C) enlève
   (D) enferme

19. Le boulanger avait . . . mon pain et a du en faire un autre.

   (A) brûlé
   (B) destiné à
   (C) établi
   (D) couvert

20. La dame a . . . le bras pour attraper le ballon.

   (A) tendu
   (B) renversé
   (C) retiré
   (D) perdu

21. L'étudiant a écrit . . . sur les œuvres de Maupassant.

   (A) une boulette
   (B) une recette
   (C) une dissertation
   (D) un témoin

22. Si nous ne rentrons pas vite chez nous, nous serons ratrappés par . . .

   (A) le pleur
   (B) la pousse
   (C) la pluie
   (D) la peur

**GO ON TO THE NEXT PAGE**

## Part B

**Directions:** Each of the following sentences contains a blank. From the four choices given, select the one that can be inserted in the blank to form a grammatically correct sentence and fill in the corresponding oval on the answer sheet. Choice (A) may consist of dashes that indicate that no insertion is required to form a grammatically correct sentence.

23. Le monsieur ------- à vous suggérer.

    (A) n'a quelque chose
    (B) n'a pas
    (C) n'a rien
    (D) a rien

24. À ------- est ce manteau vert?

    (A) que
    (B) qui
    (C) lequel
    (D) quoi

25. Je n'aime pas cette nouvelle ------- qui habite dans mon immeuble.

    (A) garçon
    (B) serveur
    (C) homme
    (D) dame

26. Aimez-vous la plage? Nous ------- allons après la classe.

    (A) en
    (B) où
    (C) y
    (D) là

27. La semaine prochaine je visite ma cousine à -------.

    (A) Mexique
    (B) France
    (C) Paris
    (D) Chine

28. Il faut toujours savoir ------- tu veux.

    (A) ce que
    (B) ce dont
    (C) a quoi
    (D) de quoi

29. Jean-Claude est venu avec -------.

    (A) ils
    (B) leur
    (C) eux
    (D) soi

30. C'est une décision ------- laquelle je vais beaucoup réfléchir.

    (A) à
    (B) sans
    (C) avec
    (D) dont

31. Elle est la personne la plus gentille que ------- jamais connue.

    (A) a
    (B) j'ai
    (C) j'aie
    (D) sois

32. Il a appris la nouvelle au moment ------- il a allumé la télé.

    (A) quand
    (B) aprés
    (C) où
    (D) durant

**GO ON TO THE NEXT PAGE**

33. Pierre ------- dehors quand le téléphone a sonné.

   (A) est
   (B) était
   (C) soit
   (D) serait

34. Nous ------- bientôt si elle a reussi son examen.

   (A) saura
   (B) saurons
   (C) saurait
   (D) savait

35. ------- les mains avant de manger!

   (A) Lavez
   (B) Brossez-vous
   (C) Serrez
   (D) Lavez-vous

36. Il n'a pas ------- signer les papiers.

   (A) décidé
   (B) le droit
   (C) envie
   (D) voulu

37. Je me ------- du souci pour votre santé.

   (A) feras
   (B) fasses
   (C) fait
   (D) faisais

38. C'est à cause de ------- que nous avons raté le train.

   (A) il
   (B) moi
   (C) se
   (D) leur

39. Est-ce que ------- cette dame qui va nous montrer la chambre?

   (A) c'est
   (B) ce soit
   (C) c'était
   (D) sera

40. Mon travail est ------- que le vôtre.

   (A) si difficile
   (B) le meilleur
   (C) pire
   (D) trop

41. N'appuyez pas trop fort sur le crayon, ------- il peut déchirer le papier.

   (A) avant que
   (B) sinon
   (C) durant
   (D) afin de

42. ------- m'a écrit.

   (A) Celui qui
   (B) Tu
   (C) C'est lui qui
   (D) Personne

**GO ON TO THE NEXT PAGE**

## Part C

**Directions:** The paragraphs below contain blank spaces indicating omissions in the text. For some blanks, it is necessary to choose the completion that is most appropriate to the meaning of the passage; for other blanks, to choose the one completion that forms a grammatically correct sentence. In some instances, choice (A) may consist of dashes that indicate that no insertion is required to form a grammatically correct sentence. In each case, indicate your answer by filling in the corresponding oval on the answer sheet. Be sure to read the paragraph completely before answering the questions related to it.

Il est trois heures et demie du matin quand j' ----(43)---- avec ma femme, sur le terrain de l'aérodrome pour le grand départ. Après avoir ----(44)---- pendant plusieurs jours un temps ----(45)----, nous sommes ----(46)---- prêts à partir ----(47)---- Tokyo. Ma femme, qui ----(48)---- née ----(49)---- Japon, n'a ----(50)---- visité la capitale, Tokyo. Elle voulait ----(51)---- y aller.

43. (A) arrivais
    (B) arriverais
    (C) arrive
    (D) étais arrivé

44. (A) attendu
    (B) attendue
    (C) attendus
    (D) attendues

45. (A) passé
    (B) mauvais
    (C) triste
    (D) favorable

46. (A) loin d'être
    (B) jamais
    (C) enfin
    (D) simplement

47. (A) dans
    (B) sans
    (C) en
    (D) pour

48. (A) était
    (B) soit
    (C) est
    (D) es

49. (A) en
    (B) au
    (C) à
    (D) dans

50. (A) toujours
    (B) pas toujours
    (C) jamais
    (D) guère

51. (A) souvent
    (B) parfois
    (C) simplement
    (D) tellement

**GO ON TO THE NEXT PAGE**

Trois ou quatre cents personnes sont là pour ----(52)---- à notre envol. Je ne sais pas comment cela se fait, ----(53)---- que nous n'avions dit à personne que nous partions. Je suis très ----(54)----, mais notre avion est très chargé et la piste est couverte de neige. Je connais bien les dangers qu'il y a à ----(55)---- dans ces conditions. Tout a été longuement ----(56)----, discuté entre nous depuis des ----(57)----, avec une très grande attention. Maintenant, j' ----(58)---- l'esprit tranquille.

52. (A) assister
    (B) assommer
    (C) asseoir
    (D) aspirer

53. (A) malgré
    (B) parce
    (C) sans
    (D) dès

54. (A) fière
    (B) énervé
    (C) calme
    (D) lourd

55. (A) débarrasser
    (B) déborder
    (C) développer
    (D) décoller

56. (A) étudié
    (B) étudier
    (C) étude
    (D) étudiant

57. (A) minutes
    (B) secondes
    (C) moments
    (D) semaines

58. (A) ai
    (B) avais
    (C) aurais
    (D) ai été

**GO ON TO THE NEXT PAGE**

## Part D

**Directions:** Read the following texts carefully for comprehension. Each is followed by a number of questions or incomplete statements. Select the completion or answer that is best according to the text and fill in the corresponding oval on the answer sheet.

Ayant laissé la voiture au garage, ils décidèrent d'attendre dans un café. Les longues files de maisons qui s'étendaient de chaque côté de la route ne formaient
*Ligne* pas un village. C'était plutôt comme un faubourg lointain
5 de Chartres, avec des maisons basses, et çà et là une devanture terne d'épicerie de campagne. Deux enfants couraient l'un après l'autre. On entendait quelqu'un frapper régulièrement une pièce de métal dans un atelier voisin. Ils se dirigèrent vers le café le plus proche.
10 C'était l'heure creuse. Il n'y avait personne. Un chat dormait sur le comptoir. Le patron apparut au bout de quelques instants, comme à regret, en traînant les jambes. Ils commandèrent n'importe quoi pour justifier leur présence. Pendant qu'il les servait, elle avait tiré
15 un poudrier de son sac et vérifiait son maquillage, machinalement. Elle était engourdie, un peu dolente, comme si on l'eût enveloppée dans une couche épaisse de coton, et les bruits ne lui parvenaient qu'assourdis. Peut-être la fatigue du voyage.
(Jean Forgère, *La Panne*, Le Livre de Poche)

59. Qu'est-ce que le couple a fait avant de chercher le café?

    (A) Ils ont attendu.
    (B) Ils ont emmené leur automobile à un garage.
    (C) Ils ont parlé avec deux enfants.
    (D) Ils ont frappé quelque chose.

60. Où se trouve le couple?

    (A) à Chartres
    (B) dans un village
    (C) dans une grande ville
    (D) dans la banlieue d'une ville

61. Quelle est la raison pour laquelle le couple est venu au café?

    (A) pour manger un bon repas
    (B) pour trouver quelqu'un avec qui ils pourraient parler
    (C) pour demander leur chemin
    (D) pour passer le temps

62. Qu'est-ce que l'auteur veut dire par l'expression "l'heure creuse"?

    (A) qu'il y avait beaucoup de monde dans le café
    (B) qu'il faisait presque nuit
    (C) que personne n'était là
    (D) que c'était l'heure où le café fermait

63. Quelle impression avait la dame au café?

    (A) qu'elle avait mangé du coton
    (B) qu'elle était trop maquillée
    (C) qu'il y avait trop de bruit
    (D) qu'elle entendait mal

**GO ON TO THE NEXT PAGE** →

Il y a, au fond de beaucoup de Français, un champion de course automobile qui sommeille et que réveille le simple contact du pied sur l'accélérateur. Le citoyen
Ligne paisible, qui vous a obligeamment invité à prendre place
5 dans sa voiture, peut se métamorphoser sous vos yeux en pilote démoniaque. Jérôme Charnelet, ce bon père de famille, qui n'écraserait pas une mouche contre une vitre, est tout prêt à écraser un piéton au kilomètre, pourvu qu'il se sente "dans son droit." Au signal vert, il voit rouge.
10 Rien ne l'arrête plus, pas même le jaune. Sur la route, cet homme, qui passe pour rangé, ne se range pas du tout. Ce n'est qu'à bout de ressources, et après avoir subi une klaxonnade nourrie, qu'il consentira de mauvaise grâce à abandonner le milieu de la chaussée.
(*L'Auto,* Hachette)

64. L'auteur écrit dans un style

(A) sérieux
(B) neutre
(C) drôle
(D) scientifique

65. Qu'est-ce qui fait apparaître le "champion de course automobile"?

(A) l'action de se mettre au volant de l'automobile
(B) le lever du soleil
(C) l'action de se réveiller
(D) un klaxon

66. D'après le passage, Jérôme Charnelet est d'habitude

(A) un champion de course
(B) d'une disposition aimable
(C) impatient
(D) généreux

67. Comment Jérôme réagit-il au signal vert?

(A) Il s'arrête.
(B) Il écrase une mouche.
(C) Il ne réussit pas à voir les couleurs.
(D) Il devient un conducteur démoniaque.

68. D'après le passage, qu'est-ce qui convaincrait Jérôme de changer de position sur la chaussée?

(A) la réalisation qu'il est au milieu de la route
(B) son sens de ses obligations envers les autres conducteurs
(C) les klaxons des autres conducteurs
(D) la couleur du signal

69. On comprend que Jérôme conduit d'une manière

(A) ordonnée
(B) rangée
(C) gracieuse
(D) obsédée

**GO ON TO THE NEXT PAGE**

## 92 HAUTS DE SEINE
### Le confort du neuf, le charme de l'ancien

Résidence "Le Valvert." Aux portes de Paris et près d'un accès autoroutier, dans immeuble du XIXe siècle, 10 appartements en cours de rénovation (du studio au 4 pièces). Parking privé dans cour intérieure. Proche du centre ville avec vue exceptionnelle sur parc aux arbres centenaires.

Prix à partir de 110000

Livraison 3ème trimestre 2005.

Bureau de vente et appartement-témoin:
01 587 45 35 12

Du lundi au samedi de 9 h 30 à 19 h, le dimanche uniquement sur rendez-vous.

70. Ces appartements

(A) vont être rénovés en 2005
(B) ont été rénovés au XIXe siècle
(C) sont en train d'être rénovés
(D) sont rénovés

71. Cette publicité s'adresse à

(A) des acheteurs éventuels
(B) de futurs locataires
(C) des personnes âgées
(D) des vendeurs

72. Après avoir lu cette publicité, on connaît tout SAUF

(A) la proximité de Paris de la résidence
(B) les heures d'ouverture du bureau de vente
(C) l'adresse exacte de la résidence
(D) l'existence d'un appartement modèle

**GO ON TO THE NEXT PAGE**

En mars 1973, un journal parisien a demandé à des jeunes de 14-15 ans quel était, pour eux, le plus mauvais moment de la journée; plus de la moitié (57%) ont
*Ligne* répondu: "Quand je pars le matin pour l'école" et 23%
5 "le temps que je passe à l'école." Tout le monde aussi le sait: beaucoup de lycéens s'ennuient; ils en ont assez, ils en ont "ras le bol." Ce sont des mots qu'on entend et qu'on lit souvent. Certains disent: "Les examens, ça sert à trouver du travail, à avoir un beau métier. Sans
10 diplôme, on ne trouve rien." Mais d'autres pensent que l'école ne sert à rien, qu'ils apprennent plus de choses à la radio, au cinéma, à la télévision ou en voyageant; et aussi que l'école est souvent coupée de la vie et qu'elle est construite, comme la société, avec des chefs, une trop
15 grande hiérarchie.
(*Les Jeunes Aujourd'hui,* Hachette)

73. Ce passage concerne

(A) le nombre d'étudiants dans le système éducatif
(B) les attitudes des adolescents français
(C) le moyen de changer l'attitude des lycéens
(D) des changements récents dans le système éducatif

74. Que veut dire l'expression "ils en ont ras le bol"?

(A) qu'ils n'ont pas assez à manger
(B) qu'ils se plaignent des études
(C) qu'ils doivent se raser
(D) qu'ils ne veulent plus de quelque chose

75. D'après l'avis de certains étudiants, où est-ce qu'on apprend le plus?

(A) en famille
(B) à l'école
(C) dans une hiérarchie
(D) dans la vie

76. Selon les étudiants qui n'aiment pas l'école, quelle est la critique la plus forte contre le système d'éducation courant?

(A) Il y a trop de travail.
(B) Les étudiants s'ennuient.
(C) Les études n'ont rien à voir avec la vie.
(D) Il n'y a pas assez de chefs.

**GO ON TO THE NEXT PAGE**

Peu après, le patron m'a fait appeler et, sur le moment, j'ai été ennuyé parce que j'ai pensé qu'il allait me dire
*Ligne* de moins téléphoner et de mieux travailler. Ce n'était pas cela du tout. Il m'a déclaré qu'il allait me parler
5 d'un projet encore très vague. Il voulait seulement avoir mon avis sur la question. Il avait l'intention d'installer un bureau à Paris qui traiterait ses affaires sur la place, et directement, avec les grandes compagnies et il voulait savoir si j'étais disposé à y aller. Cela me permettrait de
10 vivre à Paris et aussi de voyager une partie de l'année. "Vous êtes jeune, et il me semble que c'est une vie qui doit vous plaire." J'ai dit que oui mais que dans le fond cela m'était égal.
(Camus, *L'Étranger,* Folio)

77. Le narrateur s'attend à

(A) être grondé par son patron
(B) recevoir une augmentation de salaire
(C) discuter un projet avec le patron
(D) ennuyer le patron

78. Que fait le patron?

(A) Il ennuie le narrateur.
(B) Il lui commande d'aller à Paris.
(C) Il demande ce que pense le narrateur d'une suggestion.
(D) Il refuse de laisser aller le narrateur à Paris.

79. Que veut faire le patron à Paris?

(A) Il veut y habiter.
(B) Il veut travailler pour une grande compagnie.
(C) Il veut ouvrir un bureau.
(D) Il veut trahir sa compagnie.

80. Selon le passage, pour quelle raison le patron a-t-il suggéré le projet au narrateur?

(A) parce que le narrateur ne travaille pas bien
(B) parce que le patron pense que le narrateur serait content de cette vie
(C) parce que le patron est trop jeune pour le faire lui-même
(D) parce que tout est égal au narrateur

81. Quelle est la réaction du narrateur à l'idée d'aller à Paris?

(A) Il est énervé.
(B) Il est content.
(C) Il se sent rajeuni.
(D) Il ne s'y intéresse pas beaucoup.

**GO ON TO THE NEXT PAGE**

Quand une rivière est bouchée par une grosse pierre, elle attend, grossit, grossit encore. Et tout à coup la pierre saute, et l'eau, enfin libre, peut continuer son chemin. Il
*Ligne* se passe souvent la même chose dans l'histoire des arts.
5 Charles Trenet a fait sauter ce qui bouchait la chanson française, il a fait d'elle un art mais lui a donné, en même temps, une très grande liberté, liberté dans la musique, dans les paroles, et aussi dans les gestes du chanteur sur la scène. Après Trenet, il n'y a plus une chanson, il y a
10 dix, vingt, cent chansons: après lui les artistes se sentent plus libres de faire, d'écrire, de chanter, ce qu'ils veulent.
(*La Chanson Française Aujourd'hui,* Hachette)

82. Selon le passage, qu'est-ce qui rend une rivière plus grosse?

   (A) l'augmentation de l'eau qui sort de la bouche de la rivière
   (B) la présence de quelque chose qui bloque le chemin
   (C) la présence de pierres
   (D) la liberté de l'eau

83. Pourquoi l'auteur décrit-il une rivière?

   (A) pour caractériser la musique de Trenet
   (B) pour expliquer la nature
   (C) pour montrer l'importance de Trenet
   (D) pour faire une analogie avec le développement de la chanson

84. D'après ce passage, on comprend qu'avant Trenet la chanson

   (A) était plus comme une rivière
   (B) était plus compliquée
   (C) avait moins de possibilités
   (D) était plus artistique

85. On comprend que Trenet

   (A) a introduit une nouvelle façon de présenter une chanson
   (B) aimait beaucoup la nature
   (C) a écrit cent chansons
   (D) n'était pas aimé par les autres chanteurs

# S T O P
**If you finish before time is called, you may check your work on this test only.
Do not work on any other test in this book.**

# Chapter 9
# Practice Test 1:
# Answers and
# Explanations

# PRACTICE TEST 1 ANSWER KEY

| Question number | Correct answer | Right | Wrong |
|---|---|---|---|
| 1. | B | —— | —— |
| 2. | D | —— | —— |
| 3. | C | —— | —— |
| 4. | A | —— | —— |
| 5. | D | —— | —— |
| 6. | D | —— | —— |
| 7. | C | —— | —— |
| 8. | C | —— | —— |
| 9. | A | —— | —— |
| 10. | A | —— | —— |
| 11. | B | —— | —— |
| 12. | B | —— | —— |
| 13. | D | —— | —— |
| 14. | A | —— | —— |
| 15. | C | —— | —— |
| 16. | B | —— | —— |
| 17. | C | —— | —— |
| 18. | A | —— | —— |
| 19. | A | —— | —— |
| 20. | A | —— | —— |
| 21. | C | —— | —— |
| 22. | C | —— | —— |
| 23. | C | —— | —— |
| 24. | B | —— | —— |
| 25. | D | —— | —— |
| 26. | C | —— | —— |
| 27. | C | —— | —— |
| 28. | A | —— | —— |
| 29. | C | —— | —— |
| 30. | A | —— | —— |
| 31. | C | —— | —— |
| 32. | C | —— | —— |
| 33. | B | —— | —— |
| 34. | B | —— | —— |
| 35. | D | —— | —— |

| Question number | Correct answer | Right | Wrong |
|---|---|---|---|
| 36. | D | —— | —— |
| 37. | D | —— | —— |
| 38. | B | —— | —— |
| 39. | A | —— | —— |
| 40. | C | —— | —— |
| 41. | B | —— | —— |
| 42. | C | —— | —— |
| 43. | C | —— | —— |
| 44. | A | —— | —— |
| 45. | D | —— | —— |
| 46. | C | —— | —— |
| 47. | D | —— | —— |
| 48. | C | —— | —— |
| 49. | B | —— | —— |
| 50. | C | —— | —— |
| 51. | D | —— | —— |
| 52. | A | —— | —— |
| 53. | B | —— | —— |
| 54. | C | —— | —— |
| 55. | D | —— | —— |
| 56. | A | —— | —— |
| 57. | D | —— | —— |
| 58. | A | —— | —— |
| 59. | B | —— | —— |
| 60. | D | —— | —— |
| 61. | D | —— | —— |
| 62. | C | —— | —— |
| 63. | D | —— | —— |
| 64. | C | —— | —— |
| 65. | A | —— | —— |
| 66. | B | —— | —— |
| 67. | D | —— | —— |
| 68. | C | —— | —— |
| 69. | D | —— | —— |
| 70. | C | —— | —— |

| Question number | Correct answer | Right | Wrong |
|---|---|---|---|
| 71. | A | —— | —— |
| 72. | C | —— | —— |
| 73. | B | —— | —— |
| 74. | D | —— | —— |
| 75. | D | —— | —— |
| 76. | C | —— | —— |
| 77. | A | —— | —— |
| 78. | C | —— | —— |
| 79. | C | —— | —— |
| 80. | B | —— | —— |
| 81. | D | —— | —— |
| 82. | B | —— | —— |
| 83. | D | —— | —— |
| 84. | C | —— | —— |
| 85. | A | —— | —— |

# PRACTICE TEST 1 EXPLANATIONS

The possible choices are examined for clues that should have indicated the correct answer. To help explain why a choice is right or wrong, resemblances between English and French words are noted, grammatical explanations are given, and an analysis of the Comprehension questions is provided. Key words in the English translations of the questions are in **boldface**, as are the correct answers.

## Part A

| Question | | Answer | Key Word or Phrase | Fill in |
|---|---|---|---|---|
| 1 | The documents I need **for work** are still in my . . . at the office. | B | *pour mon travail* | briefcase |
| 2 | It's **nice outside**; do you want . . . after dinner? | D | *Il fait beau* (notice that these verbs, used with *te*, are reflexive) | to walk, to go outside |
| 3 | The **soldier** waited impatiently for the end of . . . | C | *soldat* | the war |
| 4 | It is not permitted to bring your dog . . . the cafe; please leave him **outside**. | A | *a l'extérieur* | into |
| 5 | Paul needs . . . **to hold up his pants**. | D | *soutenir son pantalon* | a belt, suspenders |
| 6 | For his **birthday**, the boy received many . . . | D | *anniversaire* | presents |
| 7 | The **tailor** made us new . . . . | C | *Le tailleur* | clothes |
| 8 | The . . . of my building is **564**. | C | 564 | number |
| 9 | There are **twelve** . . . **in a year**. | A | *douze, an* | months |
| 10 | The **road** is shut down; we cannot . . . anywhere. | A | *La route* | drive |
| 11 | When I wear my favorite **shoes**, I never have sore . . . | B | *souliers* | feet |
| 12 | **I agree** with him; I think that he is . . . | B | *d'accord* | right |
| 13 | The store is not . . . from my office, **so I can walk there in five minutes.** | D | *a pied en cinq minutes* | far |

| Question | | Answer | Key Word or Phrase | Fill in |
|---|---|---|---|---|
| 14 | The **hero** . . . a girl who was in the process of drowning. | A | *héros* | saved, rescued |
| 15 | In summer, one should wear . . . **to protect one's eyes.** | C | *yeux* | glasses (sun) |
| 16 | It is important . . . your teacher **questions** if you do not understand your textbook. | B | *à votre enseignant . . . si vous ne comprenez* | to ask |
| 17 | It is **not nice** . . . your friends. | C | *ce n'est pas gentil* | to be mean to, to hurt, to tease |
| 18 | The constant **noise** . . . | A | *bruit* | annoys me, upsets me |
| 19 | The baker . . . my bread and **had to make another one.** | A | *a du en faire un autre* | burned |
| 20 | The lady . . . her **arm to catch the ball.** | A | *bras, attraper* | extended, reached out |
| 21 | The student **wrote** . . . on the work of Maupassant. | C | *écrit* | an essay, a paper |
| 22 | If we do not hurry home, we will get **caught in** . . . . | C | *nous serons ratrappés par* | the rain |

## Part B

| Question | Category | Answer | Explanation |
|---|---|---|---|
| 23 | Pronouns | C | (A) no negative to go with *ne*<br>(B) no pronoun to indicate what is being suggested<br>**(C) correct: *ne* plus a negative**<br>(D) *rien* must be used with *ne* |
| 24 | Pronouns | B | (A) *que* is never used with a preposition<br>**(B) correct: *qui* can be used with prepositions**<br>(C) which—makes no sense<br>(D) what—makes no sense |
| 25 | Odds and Ends: Articles | D | (A) *garçon* would require the masculine *ce nouveau*<br>(B) *serveur* would require the masculine *ce nouveau*<br>(C) *homme* is masculine and starts with a silent "h," so would require *ce nouvel*<br>**(D) *dame* will take the feminine *cette*** |

| Question | Category | Answer | Explanation |
|----------|----------|--------|-------------|
| 26 | Pronouns | C | The required pronoun needs to refer to place or location.<br>(A) *en* will refer to location only if used with a verb that normally takes *de* (*Vient-il de là-bas? Oui, il en vient.*)<br>(B) *où* meaning "where" is used like *qui* or *que* to connect phrases<br>**(C) correct: *y* refers to place**<br>(D) *là* means "there" |
| 27 | Prepositions | C | (A) the correct expression would be *au Mexique*<br>(B) the correct expression would be *en France*<br>**(C) correct: for cities, you use *à***<br>(D) the correct expression would be *en Chine* |
| 28 | Relative Pronouns | A | **(A) *ce que* is an object of the verb *vouloir***<br>(B) *ce dont* would require a verb used with the preposition "de"<br>(C) *a quoi* would require a verb used with the preposition "a"<br>(D) *de quoi* does not fit the context of the sentence with *savoir* |
| 29 | Pronouns | C | (A) subject pronoun<br>(B) indirect object pronoun<br>**(C) correct: stressed pronoun as the object of a preposition**<br>(D) reflexive pronoun |
| 30 | Prepositions | A | **(A) correct: *réfléchir* requires *à***<br>(B) you cannot say *réfléchir sans*<br>(C) you cannot say *réfléchir avec*<br>(D) you cannot use *dont* with *laquelle* |
| 31 | Verbs | C | (A) there is no subject for the verb *avoir* here<br>(B) superlative requires the subjunctive<br>**(C) superlative requires the subjunctive**<br>(D) there is no subject for the verb *être* here |
| 32 | Pronouns | C | (A) *quand* cannot be used after *au moment*<br>(B) *après* is a preposition<br>**(C) correct: *où* is used in expressions of time**<br>(D) *durant* means during, which doesn't fit here |

| Question | Category | Answer | Explanation |
|---|---|---|---|
| 33 | Verbs | B | (A) the present doesn't work here since the other action is in the past<br>**(B) correct: imperfect—he was outside in an ongoing way in the past**<br>(C) no need for subjunctive or present<br>(D) no need for conditional |
| 34 | Verbs | B | (A) future, but third person singular<br>**(B) correct: first person plural and future**<br>(C) first person singular present conditional<br>(D) first person singular imperfect |
| 35 | Pronouns | D | (A) in this context, *laver* needs to be reflexive<br>(B) *brosser* is used for teeth, not hands<br>(C) *serrer la main*, to shake hands<br>**(D) correct: the expression is *se laver les mains*** |
| 36 | Prepositions | D | (A) *décider* takes *de*<br>(B) *avoir le droit* takes *de*<br>(C) *avoir envie* takes *de*<br>**(D) correct: *vouloir* takes a direct object** |
| 37 | Verbs | D | (A) future tense<br>(B) subjunctive form<br>(C) past participle<br>**(D) imperfect tense** |
| 38 | Pronouns | B | (A) subject pronoun<br>**(B) correct: stressed pronoun as the object of the preposition**<br>(C) reflexive pronoun<br>(D) indirect object pronoun |
| 39 | Verbs | A | **(A) correct: present**<br>(B) no need for subjunctive, as nothing is hypothetical<br>(C) imperfect cannot be used since action has not taken place yet<br>(D) the future is possible but requires *ce—ce sera* |

| Question | Category | Answer | Explanation |
|----------|----------|--------|-------------|
| 40 | Odds and Ends | C | (A) *si difficile* is not a comparative<br>(B) *le meilleur* is a superlative, not a comparative<br>**(C) correct: *pire* can be used to compare two things**<br>(D) *trop* is an adverb that needs to modify a verb, an adjective, or another adverb |
| 41 | Prepositions | B | (A) *avant que* means "before" and would require the subjunctive<br>**(B) *sinon* means "otherwise"**<br>(C) *durant* means "during"<br>(D) *afin de* means "in order to" |
| 42 | Pronouns | C | (A) this leaves the sentence incomplete<br>(B) *tu* would take the verb form *as—tu m'as écrit*<br>**(C) correct: "it is he who"**<br>(D) *personne* requires *ne* in a sentence |

## Part C

| Question | Category | Answer | Explanation |
|----------|----------|--------|-------------|
| 43 | Verbs | C | (A) imperfect indicates an ongoing action in the past<br>(B) conditional indicates one thing happening because of another<br>**(C) correct: present**<br>(D) past imperfect indicates an ongoing action that was completed in the past |
| 44 | Verbs | A | **(A) correct: no agreement**<br>(B) no need for feminine<br>(C) no need for plural<br>(D) no need for feminine plural |
| 45 | Vocabulary | D | (A) past—makes no sense<br>(B) unpleasant (i.e., bad weather)—makes no sense<br>(C) sad—makes no sense<br>**(D) correct: *favorable* (i.e., good weather)** |
| 46 | Vocabulary | C | (A) far from<br>(B) never<br>**(C) correct: finally**<br>(D) simply |

| Question | Category | Answer | Explanation |
|---|---|---|---|
| 47 | Prepositions | D | (A) you cannot say *partir dans* Tokyo<br>(B) without—makes no sense<br>(C) you cannot say *partir en* Tokyo<br>**(D) correct: *partir pour* Tokyo** |
| 48 | Verbs | C | (A) imperfect—wrong tense<br>(B) subjunctive—wrong tense<br>**(C) correct: *qui est née*. Present tense is always used when speaking about birth or death.**<br>(D) wrong person—this is the conjugation for the pronoun "tu," not "ma femme" (elle) |
| 49 | Prepositions | B | (A) you cannot say *née en Japon*<br>**(B) correct: *née au Japon (Japon* is masculine, so "*au*" is correct, not "*à la*")**<br>(C) you cannot say *née à Japon*<br>(D) you cannot say *née dans Japon* |
| 50 | Vocabulary | C | (A) always<br>(B) did not always—this does not make sense in context<br>**(C) correct: never**<br>(D) hardly |
| 51 | Odds and Ends | D | (A) often<br>(B) sometimes<br>(C) simply<br>**(D) correct: so much** |
| 52 | Vocabulary | A | **(A) correct: to attend**<br>(B) to knock down<br>(C) to sit<br>(D) to aspire, to inhale, etc. |
| 53 | Vocabulary | B | (A) in spite (of the fact)<br>**(B) correct: because—*parce que***<br>(C) without<br>(D) as soon as |
| 54 | Vocabulary | C | (A) proud<br>(B) annoyed<br>**(C) correct: calm**<br>(D) heavy |

| Question | Category | Answer | Explanation |
|---|---|---|---|
| 55 | Vocabulary | D | (A) to get rid of <br> (B) to overflow <br> (C) to develop <br> **(D) correct: to take off** |
| 56 | Odds and Ends: Adjectives | A | **(A) correct: past participle or adjective** <br> (B) verb: to study <br> (C) noun: a study <br> (D) noun: a student |
| 57 | Vocabulary | D | (A) minutes <br> (B) seconds <br> (C) moments <br> **(D) correct: weeks** |
| 58 | Verbs | A | **(A) correct: present—follows *Maintenant*** <br> (B) imperfect <br> (C) conditional <br> (D) *passé composé* |

## Part D

| Question | | Answer | Explanation |
|---|---|---|---|
| 59 | What did the couple do before looking for the café? | B | (A) "They waited." <br> **(B) "They took their car to a garage.": correct—another way of saying *Ayant laissé la voiture au garage . . .*** <br> (C) "They spoke to two children.": familiar words—wrong context <br> (D) "They hit something.": familiar words—wrong context |
| 60 | Where is the couple? | D | (A) *À Chartres*: familiar words—wrong context <br> (B) "in a village": *ne formaient pas un village* <br> (C) "in a big town": common sense—if it's not even a village, it's certainly not a city <br> **(D) "in a suburb of the town": correct—key words are *un faubourg lointain*** |

| Question | | Answer | Explanation |
|---|---|---|---|
| 61 | For what reason did the couple go to the café? | D | (A) "to eat a good meal": no, since *Ils commandèrent n'importe quoi pour justifier leur présence.*<br>(B) "to find someone to talk to": no context for this<br>(C) "to ask directions": no context for this<br>**(D) "to pass the time": correct—*ils décidèrent d'attendre dans un café* |
| 62 | What does the author mean by "*l'heure creuse*"? | C | (A) "that there were a lot of people in the café": incorrect—the café was empty<br>(B) "that it was almost night": no context for this<br>**(C) "that no one was there": correct—*Il n'y avait personne.***<br>(D) "that it was time for the café to close": no context for this |
| 63 | What impression did the lady have at the café? | D | (A) "that she had eaten cotton": familiar words—wrong context<br>(B) "that she had on too much makeup": familiar words—wrong context<br>(C) "that there was too much noise": familiar words—wrong context<br>**(D) "that she couldn't hear": correct—*les bruits ne lui parvenaient qu'assourdis*** |
| 64 | The author writes in a style that is | C | (A) "serious"<br>(B) "neutral": the author is obviously doing more than just describing the scene<br>**(C) "humorous": correct—tip-offs are word play (*rangé, se range*), exaggeration**<br>(D) "scientific" |
| 65 | What makes the race car driver appear? | A | **(A) "the act of getting behind the wheel":** *et que réveille le simple contact du pied sur l'accélérateur*<br>(B) "the sunrise"<br>(C) "the action of waking up"<br>(D) "a horn": familiar word—*klaxonner*—but wrong context |

| Question | | Answer | Explanation |
|---|---|---|---|
| 66 | According to the passage, Jérôme Charnelet is usually | B | (A) "a race car driver": familiar words—wrong context<br>(B) **"of an amiable disposition": correct—*ce bon père de famille* . . .**<br>(C) "impatient"<br>(D) "generous" |
| 67 | How does Jérôme react to the green light? | D | (A) "He stops.": makes no sense<br>(B) "He swats a fly.": familiar words—wrong context<br>(C) "He has trouble seeing colors.": you're interpreting too literally<br>(D) **"He becomes a crazy driver.": correct—*il voit rouge*** |
| 68 | What would convince Jérôme to change his position on the road? | C | (A) "the realization that he is in the middle of the road": familiar words—wrong context<br>(B) "his sense of obligation to the other drivers": familiar words—wrong context<br>(C) **"the horns of other drivers": correct—*après avoir subi une klaxonnade nourrie* . . . "After having been subjected to continuous honking . . . "**<br>(D) "the color of the traffic light": familiar words—wrong context |
| 69 | We understand that Jérôme drives in a manner that is | D | (A) "orderly"<br>(B) "steady": familiar word—*rangée*—but wrong context<br>(C) "gracious"<br>(D) **"obsessed": correct—*obsédée*; the key word is *démoniaque*** |
| 70 | These apartments | C | (A) "will be renovated in 2005"—no context for this<br>(B) "were renovated in the 19th century"—familiar words—wrong context<br>(C) **"are being renovated": correct—"*en cours de rénovation*"**<br>(D) "are renovated" |
| 71 | This advertisement is aimed at | A | (A) **"prospective buyers": correct—"*bureau de vente*"**<br>(B) "future tenants"—no context for this<br>(C) "elderly people"—no context for this<br>(D) "sellers"—familiar word—wrong context |

| Question | | Answer | Explanation |
|---|---|---|---|
| 72 | After reading this advertisement, one is aware of everything BUT | C | (A) "the proximity of Paris to the residence"—*aux portes de Paris*<br>(B) "the opening hours of the sales office"—*du lundi au samedi de 9 h 30 à 19 h*<br>**(C) "the precise address of the residence": correct—this is the only thing one does not know about these apartments**<br>(D) "the existence of a show apartment"—*appartement-témoin* |
| 73 | This passage is concerned with | B | (A) "the number of students in the educational system": incorrect—percentages are given, not numbers<br>**(B) "the attitudes of French adolescents": correct**<br>(C) "the way to change the attitude of French students": no context for this<br>(D) "recent changes in the educational system": no context for this |
| 74 | What does the expression "*ils en ont ras le bol*" mean? | D | (A) "that they do not have enough to eat"<br>(B) "that they complain about their studies"<br>(C) "that they should shave"<br>**(D) "that they are sick and tired of something": correct—*ils en ont assez*** |
| 75 | According to certain students, where does one learn the most? | D | (A) "at home": no context for this<br>(B) "at school": obviously incorrect<br>(C) "in a hierarchy": incorrect—this is one of the problems<br>**(D) "in life": correct—*à la radio, au cinéma, à la télévision ou en voyageant . . .*** |
| 76 | What is the strongest criticism of the educational system? | C | (A) "There is too much work.": no context for this<br>(B) "The students are bored.": a concern, but not the biggest problem<br>**(C) correct: *l'école est souvent coupée de la vie . . .* "school is often cut off from life . . ."**<br>(D) "There are not enough bosses.": just the opposite |

| Question | | Answer | Explanation |
|---|---|---|---|
| 77 | The narrator expects | A | (A) **"to be scolded by his boss"**: correct—*j'ai pensé qu'il allait me dire de moins téléphoner et de mieux travailler*<br>(B) "to get a raise": no context for this<br>(C) "to discuss a project with his boss": no context for this<br>(D) "to annoy the boss": familiar words—wrong context |
| 78 | What does the boss do? | C | (A) "He annoys the narrator.": familiar words—wrong context<br>(B) "He orders him to go to Paris.": too strong—the boss asks if he wants to go<br>(C) **"He asks what the narrator thinks of a suggestion."**: correct—*Il voulait seulement avoir mon avis sur la question*<br>(D) "He refuses to let the narrator go to Paris.": wrong |
| 79 | What does the boss want to do in Paris? | C | (A) "He wants to live there.": perhaps, but too vague to be a good answer<br>(B) "He wants to work for a big company.": familiar words—wrong context<br>(C) **"He wants to open an office."**: correct—*l'intention d'installer un bureau à Paris . . .*<br>(D) "He wishes to betray his company.": no evidence for this |
| 80 | Why does the boss suggest the project to the narrator? | B | (A) "because the narrator isn't working well": no, the narrator is evidently being rewarded<br>(B) **"because he thinks the narrator would be happy with such a life"**: correct—*il me semble que c'est une vie qui doit vous plaire*<br>(C) "because the boss is too young to do it himself": familiar words—but misleading<br>(D) "because it's all the same to the narrator": familiar words—wrong context |
| 81 | What reaction does the narrator have to the idea of going to Paris? | D | (A) "He is irritated.": no context for this<br>(B) "He is happy.": he is neither happy nor unhappy<br>(C) "He feels rejuvenated.": no context for this<br>(D) **"He's not very interested."**: correct—*dans le fond cela m'était égal* |

| Question | | Answer | Explanation |
|---|---|---|---|
| 82 | What makes a river bigger? | B | (A) "an increase in water that comes from the mouth of the river": familiar words—wrong context<br>**(B) "the presence of something that blocks the way": correct—*Quand une rivière est bouchée par une grosse pierre . . .***<br>(C) "the presence of rocks": familiar words—wrong context<br>(D) "the freedom of water": familiar words—wrong context |
| 83 | Why does the author describe a river? | D | (A) "to characterize Trenet's music": not in this case<br>(B) "to explain nature": makes no sense<br>(C) "to show Trenet's importance": tricky—but not an answer to this question<br>**(D) "to make an analogy with the development of song": correct—*Il se passe souvent la même chose dans l'histoire des arts.*** |
| 84 | It is inferred that before Trenet, the song (in this context, *la chanson* means songs in general) | C | (A) "was more like a river": makes no sense<br>(B) "was more complicated": no context for this<br>**(C) "had fewer possibilities": correct—*après lui les artistes se sentent plus libres . . .***<br>(D) "was more artistic": no context for this |
| 85 | One can infer that Trenet | A | **(A) "introduced a new way of presenting a song": correct—*Charles Trenet a fait sauter ce qui bouchait la chanson française . . .***<br>(B) "loved nature": makes no sense<br>(C) "wrote a hundred songs": familiar words but wrong context<br>(D) "wasn't liked by other singers": no context for this |

# HOW TO SCORE PRACTICE TEST 1

When you take the real exam, the proctors will collect your test booklet and answer sheet and send your answer sheet to a processing center where a computer looks at the pattern of filled-in ovals on your answer sheet and gives you a score. We are providing you, however, with this more primitive way of scoring your exam.

## Determining Your Score

**STEP 1**  Using the answer key, determine how many questions you got right and how many you got wrong on the test. Remember: Questions that you do not answer do not count as either right answers or wrong answers.

**STEP 2**  Write the number of correct answers on line A.

(A) _____

**STEP 3**  Write the number of wrong answers on line B. Divide that number by 3.

(B) _____ ÷ 3 = _____

**STEP 4**  Subtract the number of wrong answers divided by 3 on line B from the number of correct answers on line A, and round to the nearest whole number. (C) is your **raw score**.

(A) _____ – (B) _____ = (C) _____

**STEP 5**  To determine your **real score**, look up your raw score in the left column of the Score Conversion Table on the next page; the corresponding score on the right is the score you earned on the exam.

# PRACTICE TEST 1
## SCORE CONVERSION TABLE

| Raw score | Scaled score | Raw score | Scaled score | Raw score | Scaled score |
|-----------|-----------|-----------|-----------|-----------|-----------|
| 85 | 800 | 45 | 630 | 5 | 410 |
| 84 | 800 | 44 | 620 | 4 | 410 |
| 83 | 800 | 43 | 620 | 3 | 400 |
| 82 | 800 | 42 | 610 | 2 | 400 |
| 81 | 800 | 41 | 610 | 1 | 390 |
| 80 | 800 | 40 | 600 | 0 | 390 |
| 79 | 800 | 39 | 600 | −1 | 380 |
| 78 | 800 | 38 | 590 | −2 | 380 |
| 77 | 800 | 37 | 580 | −3 | 370 |
| 76 | 790 | 36 | 580 | −4 | 360 |
| 75 | 790 | 35 | 570 | −5 | 360 |
| 74 | 780 | 34 | 570 | −6 | 350 |
| 73 | 780 | 33 | 560 | −7 | 350 |
| 72 | 770 | 32 | 560 | −8 | 340 |
| 71 | 770 | 31 | 550 | −9 | 340 |
| 70 | 760 | 30 | 550 | −10 | 330 |
| 69 | 760 | 29 | 540 | −11 | 330 |
| 68 | 750 | 28 | 540 | −12 | 320 |
| 67 | 740 | 27 | 530 | −13 | 320 |
| 66 | 740 | 26 | 530 | −14 | 310 |
| 65 | 730 | 25 | 520 | −15 | 300 |
| 64 | 730 | 24 | 520 | −16 | 290 |
| 63 | 720 | 23 | 510 | −17 | 290 |
| 62 | 720 | 22 | 500 | −18 | 280 |
| 61 | 710 | 21 | 500 | −19 | 280 |
| 60 | 710 | 20 | 490 | −20 | 270 |
| 59 | 700 | 19 | 490 | −21 | 270 |
| 58 | 700 | 18 | 480 | −22 | 260 |
| 57 | 690 | 17 | 480 | −23 | 260 |
| 56 | 690 | 16 | 470 | −24 | 250 |
| 55 | 680 | 15 | 470 | −25 through −28 | 240 |
| 54 | 680 | 14 | 460 | | |
| 53 | 670 | 13 | 460 | | |
| 52 | 660 | 12 | 450 | | |
| 51 | 660 | 11 | 450 | | |
| 50 | 650 | 10 | 440 | | |
| 49 | 650 | 9 | 430 | | |
| 48 | 640 | 8 | 430 | | |
| 47 | 640 | 7 | 420 | | |
| 46 | 630 | 6 | 420 | | |

# Chapter 10
# Practice Test 2

# FRENCH SUBJECT TEST 2

When your supervisor gives the signal, turn the page and begin the SAT French Subject Test.

# FRENCH SUBJECT TEST 2

PLEASE NOTE THAT YOUR ANSWER SHEET HAS FIVE ANSWER POSITIONS MARKED A, B, C, D, E, WHILE THE QUESTIONS THROUGHOUT THIS TEST CONTAIN ONLY FOUR CHOICES. BE SURE <u>NOT</u> TO MAKE ANY MARKS IN COLUMN E.

## Part A

**Directions:** This part consists of a number of incomplete statements, each having four suggested completions. Select the most appropriate completion and fill in the corresponding oval on the answer sheet.

1. Les étudiants sont . . . avec l'enseignant sur l'explication de l'examen.

   (A) en retard
   (B) d'accord
   (C) a l'heure
   (D) avant de

2. N'oublie pas ton parapluie; il va . . . ce soir.

   (A) pleurer
   (B) faire froid
   (C) ouvrir
   (D) pleuvoir

3. Il n'y a plus rien dans le réfrigérateur. Il faut que j'aille . . .

   (A) prendre une douche
   (B) tondre le gazon
   (C) faire les courses
   (D) mettre le couvert

4. J'ai mal à . . . d'avoir tapé à l'ordinateur toute la journée.

   (A) la main
   (B) le pied
   (C) l'oreille
   (D) la barbe

5. Sa voiture est toujours en panne et il en a vraiment . . .

   (A) marre
   (B) mer
   (C) miel
   (D) dégoûté

6. Au crépuscule, le ciel . . . de mille feux.

   (A) éteignait
   (B) disparaissait
   (C) tombait
   (D) brillait

7. Les engagements . . . doivent être honores; sinon les gens ne vont pas faire confiance en vous.

   (A) être pauvre
   (B) reçu
   (C) pris
   (D) recueillir

8. Jean va acheter des livres à la . . .

   (A) boucherie
   (B) librairie
   (C) pâtisserie
   (D) bibliothèque

9. Elle est si allergique à la poussière qu'elle . . . sans arrêt.

   (A) éclate
   (B) éclabousse
   (C) éternue
   (D) embrasse

10. J'ai ouvert une nouvelle . . . dans le centre de la ville ou je vends des gâteaux.

   (A) entreprise
   (B) une gare
   (C) champ de bataille
   (D) voilier

**GO ON TO THE NEXT PAGE**

11. Il s'est évanoui en apprenant . . .

   (A) la nouvelle
   (B) la leçon
   (C) le fauteuil
   (D) la poubelle

12. Personne ne répond à la porte; elle n'est probablement pas . . .

   (A) là
   (B) dessus
   (C) dessous
   (D) à côté

13. Je suis très . . . que le garçon prend tellement de temps avec ma commande.

   (A) heureux
   (B) satisfait; je suis presse
   (C) fâché
   (D) ravi

14. Ils ont choisi d'habiter . . . avec leurs trois petits enfants.

   (A) en banlieue
   (B) en chemin
   (C) en cachette
   (D) en retard

15. Ils sont pleins d'énergie et sont . . . tous les matins à 6 heures.

   (A) étendus
   (B) assis
   (C) debout
   (D) fâchés

16. Je n'ai pas . . . d'acheter une nouvelle voiture je peux me déplacer à vélo en ville.

   (A) hésiter
   (B) espoir
   (C) hésiter
   (D) besoin

17. Pour son entrevue avec son futur employeur demain, elle va mettre . . .

   (A) un soulier
   (B) un tailleur
   (C) un costume
   (D) un portemanteau

18. Elle a . . . beaucoup d'argent pour acheter sa maison.

   (A) prêté
   (B) renversé
   (C) emprunté
   (D) vendu

19. Je suppose que vous . . . parce que la journée a été très chaude.

   (A) avez soif
   (B) avez progreseé
   (C) avez détruit
   (D) avez évoqué

20. Il est exténué; il a . . . travaillé.

   (A) peu
   (B) bientôt
   (C) souvent
   (D) trop

21. Les trains passent moins souvent les jours . . .

   (A) normaux
   (B) libres
   (C) fériés
   (D) courants

22. Cette ancienne carte va nous . . . où le trésor est enterré.

   (A) masquer
   (B) montrer
   (C) rappeler
   (D) demander

**GO ON TO THE NEXT PAGE**

23. Des années d'usage vont . . . le cuir de ces bottes.

    (A) assiéger
    (B) réduire
    (C) assouplir
    (D) surprendre

24. Si je pars maintenant, je peux . . . les embouteillages.

    (A) estimer
    (B) revoir
    (C) arranger
    (D) éviter

**GO ON TO THE NEXT PAGE**

## Part B

**Directions:** Each of the following sentences contains a blank. From the four choices given, select the one that can be inserted in the blank to form a grammatically correct sentence and fill in the corresponding oval on the answer sheet. Choice (A) may consist of dashes that indicate that no insertion is required to form a grammatically correct sentence.

25. Le paquet ------- mon père a signé est sur la table de la cuisine.

    (A) que
    (B) à qui
    (C) pour lequel
    (D) dont

26. Je suis passée à la maison ------- prendre mon parapluie.

    (A) à
    (B) pour
    (C) parce que
    (D) après

27. Mon père revenait toujours ------- à la maison entre midi et deux heures.

    (A) déjeuner
    (B) déjeuné
    (C) déjeunait
    (D) déjeunant

28. Les chocolats ------- Belgique sont les meilleurs au monde.

    (A) de la
    (B) dans
    (C) aux
    (D) du

29. Elle dessine beaucoup ------- que son frère.

    (A) bien
    (B) meilleur
    (C) mal
    (D) mieux

30. La robe qu'elle a ------- hier n'est vraiment pas à la mode.

    (A) mise
    (B) acheté
    (C) mis
    (D) enfiler

31. ------- quelqu'un d'autre a faim, on va fermer la cuisine pour ce soir.

    (A) Avant que
    (B) Puisque
    (C) Bien que
    (D) À moins que

32. Regarde ------- tu mets les pieds quand tu marches.

    (A) là
    (B) où
    (C) vers
    (D) près de

**GO ON TO THE NEXT PAGE**

33. Appelle-moi ------- prendre une décision.

    (A) en
    (B) pendant
    (C) avant de
    (D) à

34. ------- mieux prendre des vacances plutôt que de rester à la maison en hiver.

    (A) Je vais aimer
    (B) J'aimais
    (C) J'aimerais
    (D) Que j'aime

35. Est-ce que tu veux un bonbon? Oui, j'en veux bien -------.

    (A) quelque
    (B) peu
    (C) un peu
    (D) un

36. Est-ce que Marie est déjà partie à la poste? Non, mais elle va ------- aller tout de suite.

    (A) y
    (B) en
    (C) toujours
    (D) demain

37. Il ------- tous les jours avant de dejeuner quand il etait en vacances.

    (A) va nager
    (B) avait nagé
    (C) a nagé
    (D) serait nager

38. Il faut que ------- à la banque demain matin pour retirer de l'argent.

    (A) j'allais
    (B) j'aille
    (C) j'irai
    (D) j'irais

**GO ON TO THE NEXT PAGE**

## Part C

**Directions:** The paragraphs below contain blank spaces indicating omissions in the text. For some blanks, it is necessary to choose the completion that is most appropriate to the meaning of the passage; for other blanks, to choose the one completion that forms a grammatically correct sentence. In some instances, choice (A) may consist of dashes that indicate that no insertion is required to form a grammatically correct sentence. In each case, indicate your answer by filling in the corresponding oval on the answer sheet. Be sure to read the paragraph completely before answering the questions related to it.

Il n'avait pas mangé ----(39)---- le matin. Les cafés qu'il rencontrait à ----(40)---- pas l'intimidaient et ----(41)---- dégoûtaient, à cause de la foule qui ----(42)---- était ----(43)----. Il s'adressa ----(44)---- un gendarme. Mais il était si lent à ----(45)---- ses mots que l'autre ne se donna même pas la peine de l'écouter ----(46)---- bout et lui tourna ----(47)----, au milieu de la phrase, en ----(48)---- les épaules. Il continua machinalement ----(49)---- marcher.

39. (A) après
    (B) depuis
    (C) pour
    (D) dans

40. (A) tous
    (B) chacun
    (C) chaque
    (D) quelque

41. (A) lui
    (B) la
    (C) le
    (D) leur

42. (A) en
    (B) y
    (C) dans
    (D) où

43. (A) entassé
    (B) entasser
    (C) entassées
    (D) entassée

44. (A) à
    (B) vers
    (C) avec
    (D) pour

45. (A) trouvé
    (B) trouver
    (C) trouvés
    (D) trouvait

46. (A) à travers
    (B) jusque-là
    (C) au
    (D) jusqu'au

47. (A) la tête
    (B) le dos
    (C) l'oreille
    (D) les yeux

48. (A) tirant
    (B) portant
    (C) haussant
    (D) passant

49. (A) -------
    (B) pour
    (C) à
    (D) en

GO ON TO THE NEXT PAGE

Cher Monsieur,

La lettre ----(50)---- je vous ----(51)---- adressée le 1er juillet ----(52)---- restée sans réponse, je me permets de vous écrire pour ----(53)---- prier de prendre ma requête ----(54)---- considération.

50. (A) -------
(B) laquelle
(C) dont
(D) que

53. (A) te
(B) me
(C) vous
(D) le

51. (A) aie
(B) ai
(C) aurai
(D) avait

54. (A) en
(B) avec
(C) par
(D) comme

52. (A) ayant
(B) avant
(C) étant
(D) était

Quand j'étais petit, mes parents ----(55)---- emmenaient ----(56)---- nager à la piscine municipale de Roubaix.

55. (A) leur
(B) te
(C) s'
(D) m'

56. (A) peut-être
(B) pourtant
(C) une fois
(D) souvent

**GO ON TO THE NEXT PAGE**

## Part D

**Directions:** Read the following texts carefully for comprehension. Each is followed by a number of questions or incomplete statements. Select the completion or answer that is best according to the text and fill in the corresponding oval on the answer sheet.

"L'été est trop long," disait la grand-mère qui accueillait du même soupir soulagé la pluie d'automne et le départ de Jacques, dont les piétinements d'ennui

*Ligne* au long des journées torrides, dans les pièces aux
5 persiennes closes, ajoutaient encore à son énervement.
Elle ne comprenait pas d'ailleurs qu'une période de l'année fût plus spécialement désignée pour n'y rien faire. "Je n'ai jamais eu de vacances, moi," disait-elle, et c'était vrai, elle n'avait connu ni l'école
10 ni le loisir, elle avait travaillé enfant, et travaillé sans relâche. Elle admettait que, pour un bénéfice plus grand, son petit-fils pendant quelques années ne rapporte pas d'argent à la maison. Mais, dès le premier jour, elle avait commencé de ruminer sur
15 ces trois mois perdus, et, lorsque Jacques entra en troisième, elle jugea qu'il était temps de lui trouver l'emploi de ses vacances. "Tu vas travailler cet été," lui dit-elle à la fin de l'année scolaire,"et rapporter un peu d'argent à la maison. Tu ne peux pas rester
20 comme ça sans rien faire."

(Albert Camus, *Le premier homme*, Folio)

57. Quand arrivait la pluie d'automne, la grand-mère était

    (A) énervée
    (B) triste
    (C) contente
    (D) fière

58. Pendant les mois d'été, Jacques

    (A) travaillait beaucoup
    (B) passait son temps à lire
    (C) s'amusait sans arrêt
    (D) ne savait pas comment se distraire

59. Quand elle était petite, la grand-mère

    (A) avait de moins longues vacances que Jacques
    (B) dessinait pendant ses loisirs
    (C) passait tout son temps au travail
    (D) ne faisait jamais rien

60. D'après le texte, on comprend que

    (A) Jacques poursuit ses études
    (B) la grand-mère ne veut pas que Jacques aille encore à l'école
    (C) la grand-mère refuse que Jacques travaille pendant l'été
    (D) Jacques est le troisième de sa classe

61. La grand-mère veut que Jacques ait un emploi pour qu'il

    (A) ait un peu d'argent de poche
    (B) puisse payer ses études
    (C) contribue aux dépenses de la famille
    (D) apprenne un métier

**GO ON TO THE NEXT PAGE**

Avant de venir au Central, lisait-il, je viens
d'assister à une scène d'une atroce beauté.

*Ligne*    On a trouvé cette nuit près de la Puerta del Sol un
enfant de trois ans qui pleurait perdu, dans les ténèbres.
5 Or, une des femmes réfugiées dans les sous-sols de
la Gran Via ignorait ce qu'était devenu son enfant,
un petit garçon du même âge, blond comme l'enfant
trouvé dans la Puerta del Sol. On lui donne la nouvelle.
Elle court à la maison où l'on garde l'enfant, calle
10 Montera. Dans la demi-obscurité d'une boutique aux
rideaux baissés, l'enfant suce un morceau de chocolat.
La mère s'avance vers lui, les bras tendus, mais ses
yeux s'agrandissent, prennent une fixité terrible,
démente.
15 Ce n'est pas son enfant.
Elle reste immobile de longues minutes. L'enfant
perdu lui sourit. Alors elle se précipite sur lui, le serre
contre elle, l'emporte en pensant à l'enfant qu'on n'a
pas retrouvé.

(André Malraux, *L'espoir*, Folio Plus)

62. L'enfant de trois ans pleure parce qu'

(A) il a perdu son morceau de chocolat
(B) il s'est fait mal
(C) il ne sait pas où est sa famille
(D) il fait nuit

63. Les rideaux de la boutique sont

(A) ouverts
(B) levés
(C) descendus
(D) déchirés

64. La femme "se précipite sur lui" veut dire qu'elle
va vers l'enfant

(A) en courant
(B) à pas lents
(C) en pleurant
(D) avec nonchalance

65. Elle "le serre contre elle" signifie qu'elle

(A) le repousse
(B) l'embrasse
(C) lui sourit
(D) le frappe

66. A qui la femme pense-t-elle en emportant l'enfant?

(A) à son propre fils
(B) au fils d'une des refugiées
(C) au fils du lecteur
(D) au fils d'un garde

**GO ON TO THE NEXT PAGE**

## TRAIN + VOITURE: EN TOUTE LIBERTÉ

**Evitez les bouchons des grands départs!**

En choisissant la formule "Train + Location de voitures," vous êtes sûrs de bénéficier de tous les avantages: le confort du train, la liberté de la voiture … Tout en réalisant de vraies **économies**!

**Pratique**: à la descente du train, votre voiture vous attend en gare.

**Economique**: vous bénéficiez d'une réduction importante sur votre location.

**Efficace**: vous réservez votre voiture en même temps que votre train.

Pour profiter de cette offre:

– Réservez votre place.

– En fin de commande, cliquez sur "AJOUTER UNE VOITURE."

– Choisissez l'offre "Train + Location de Voitures."

67. Les bouchons dont il est question dans le texte

 (A) servent à boucher les bouteilles
 (B) sont des embouteillages
 (C) retardent les trains
 (D) évitent de perdre du temps

68. D'après le texte, la solution Train + Location de Voitures

 (A) revient plus cher
 (B) coûte trop cher
 (C) n'est guère pratique
 (D) est une bonne affaire

**GO ON TO THE NEXT PAGE**

Les Français auraient-ils attrapé le virus du home cinéma ? A en croire la grande majorité des constructeurs d'électronique grand public, la réponse ne fait pas de doute. Les équipements liés au cinéma à domicile, qui englobent aussi bien de la hi-fi que de la vidéo, ont le vent en poupe. Tous les professionnels du secteur s'accordent même pour dire que 2002 devrait être l'année de l'explosion de ce marché en France. Près de 4 millions de téléviseurs, dont 15% avec un écran au format cinéma 16/9, devraient ainsi être vendus en 2002 selon les prévisions de l'institut GFK.

"Il y a toujours eu en France une forte sensibilité des gens à consommer des films à la maison," explique Jean-Marc Auffret, responsable marketing home cinéma chez Sony France. "Mais jusqu'à présent le home cinéma était réservé à une frange très cinéphile et relativement aisée financièrement. Aujourd'hui, avec l'apparition des appareils combinés et la baisse des prix de certains éléments audiovisuels, le grand public peut plus facilement s'équipper." Il est sans doute encore trop tôt pour parler de démocratisation— installer un ensemble home cinéma coûte toujours entre 1300 et plus de 60000 euros selon les matériels choisis—mais les constructeurs disposent de plus en plus de produits abordables. Aujourd'hui, il est possible d'acheter un ensemble composé d'un lecteur de DVD équipé d'un amplificateur et d'un pack de six enceintes pour moins de 700 euros.

(Guillaume Fraissard, *Le Monde*, 31 mai, 2002)

69. D'après cet article, les Français

(A) vont de plus en plus souvent au cinéma
(B) vont rarement au cinéma
(C) préfèrent regarder la télévision
(D) aiment de plus en plus regarder des films chez eux

70. Les équipements liés au cinéma à domicile

(A) ont de plus en plus de succès
(B) ne sont pas nouveaux
(C) n'ont guère d'intérêt
(D) ne sont pas dans le vent

71. Aujourd'hui, l'audiovisuel est

(A) plus coûteux
(B) meilleur marché
(C) hors de prix
(D) inabordable

72. "Le grand public" représente

(A) quelques privilégiés
(B) les gens célèbres
(C) les amateurs de cinéma
(D) la plupart des gens

73. " . . . les constructeurs disposent de plus en plus de produits abordables" signifie qu'ils

(A) s'en débarrassent
(B) en ont besoin
(C) y ont accès
(D) en fabriquent

**GO ON TO THE NEXT PAGE**

Voici la recette des madeleines, ces petits gâteaux de forme ovale au ventre bombé, si chers à Marcel Proust:

La veille, mélangez soigneusement les ingrédients suivants jusqu'à l'obtention d'une pâte parfaitement lisse:

### Madeleines

| | |
|---|---|
| Farine | 90 gr |
| Sucre | 90 gr |
| Levure | 2 gr |
| Miel de Provence | 10 gr |
| Oeufs | 2 |
| Beurre fondu | 90 gr |
| Le zeste d'un citron | |
| Pastis (facultatif) | 1 cl |

Conservez cette pâte au réfrigérateur.

Le lendemain, distribuez la pâte dans 12 moules à madeleines beurrés. Enfournez à four moyen et laissez cuire jusqu'à ce que les gâteaux aient une belle couleur dorée. Démoulez sur une grille à la sortie du four, laissez refroidir, et dégustez!

74. Quand faut-il préparer la pâte des madeleines?

(A) le lendemain
(B) le jour précédent
(C) deux heures à l'avance
(D) hier

75. D'après la recette, le pastis est un ingrédient

(A) indispensable
(B) sucré
(C) optionnel
(D) parfumé

**GO ON TO THE NEXT PAGE**

Le bossu reparut, une brochure à la main. Il s'installa commodément, les coudes sur la table, son menton entre ses mains.

*Ligne*
"Je vous ai déjà laissé entendre, dit-il, que j'avais
5 des projets d'une assez grande envergure."

"De vastes projets."

"C'est cela même, et je vais vous les révéler aujourd'hui." Il prit le ton d'un conférencier.

"Ce qui m'a attiré ici, c'est d'abord mon amour
10 de la nature. Mais quoique je ne manque pas d'argent en ce moment, j'ai une famille à nourrir, et je dois assurer l'avenir de ma fillette: c'est pourquoi le philosophe que je suis a voulu concilier son désir de la vie naturelle et l'obligation où il se trouve de faire
15 fortune."

De ce discours, Ugolin ne retint que les derniers mots. Il avait l'intention de "faire fortune." Faire fortune aux Romarins! Avec quoi? Sûrement pas avec ces oliviers à demi morts, ni ces amandiers à l'agonie;
20 ni avec des légumes, ni avec du blé, ni avec du vin. Il connaissait donc la source, et il voulait peut-être planter des œillets! C'est pourquoi, par une contre-attaque désespérée, il dit: "Vous savez ici, les fleurs, même si vous aviez une belle source . . ."
25 "Quelles fleurs?" dit le bossu d'un air surpris. "Croyez-vous que j'espère faire fortune en vendant des églantines ou des chardons? Et quelle source? Vous savez que celle que je possède est bien loin d'ici!"

(Marcel Pagnol, *Jean de Florette*, Presses Pocket)

76. "Je vous ai déjà laissé entendre" signifie "je vous ai déjà"

(A) dit
(B) répété
(C) suggéré
(D) menti

77. Le bossu a de "vastes projets" parce qu'il

(A) a besoin d'argent tout de suite
(B) pense à l'avenir de sa fille
(C) est philosophe
(D) aime beaucoup l'argent

78. Du discours du bossu, Ugolin se souvient

(A) uniquement des derniers mots
(B) peut-être des premiers mots
(C) toujours de la dernière phrase
(D) de tout sauf de la fin

79. Aux lignes 18–23, apres l'annonce des projets du bossu, Ugolin est

(A) amusé
(B) très inquiet
(C) rempli de joie
(D) rassuré

80. Ugolin cherche à savoir si le bossu

(A) va planter des vignes
(B) va sauver les oliviers et les amandiers
(C) compte vendre des chardons
(D) connaît l'existence de la source

**GO ON TO THE NEXT PAGE** →

*Ligne*

Vous comprenez tout de suite que la vraie ville est
l'arsenal, que l'autre ne vit que par lui, qu'il déborde
sur elle. Sous toutes les formes, en tous lieux, à tous
les coins réapparaissent l'administration, la discipline,
5 la feuille de papier rayé, le cadre, la règle. On admire
beaucoup la symétrie factice et la propreté imbécile.
A l'hôpital de la marine, par exemple, les salles sont
cirées de telle façon qu'un convalescent, essayant de
marcher sur sa jambe remise, doit se casser l'autre
10 en tombant. Mais c'est beau, ça brille, on s'y mire.
Entre chaque salle est une cour, mais où le soleil ne
vient jamais et dont soigneusement on arrache l'herbe.
Les cuisines sont superbes, mais à une telle distance,
qu'en hiver tout doit parvenir glacé aux malades. Il
15 s'agit bien d'eux! Les casseroles ne sont-elles pas
luisantes? Nous vîmes un homme qui s'était cassé le
crâne en tombant d'une frégate et qui depuis dix-huit
heures n'avait pas encore reçu de secours; mais ses
draps étaient très blancs, car la lingerie est fort bien
20 tenue.

(Gustave Flaubert, *Notes de voyage*, L'Intégrale)

81. "En tous lieux" signifie

(A) nulle part
(B) partout
(C) ailleurs
(D) quelque part

82. Le convalescent risque de se casser l'autre jambe
parce que le sol est

(A) mouillé
(B) inégal
(C) plein de trous
(D) glissant

83. La cour entre chaque salle est

(A) inondée de soleil
(B) privée d'ombre
(C) ensoleillée
(D) privée de soleil

84. En hiver les repas sont servis aux malades

(A) brûlants
(B) tièdes
(C) à point
(D) très froids

85. Le ton de Flaubert dans ce passage est

(A) sarcastique
(B) sérieux
(C) enjoué
(D) tragique

# S T O P
**If you finish before time is called, you may check your work on this test only.
Do not work on any other test in this book.**

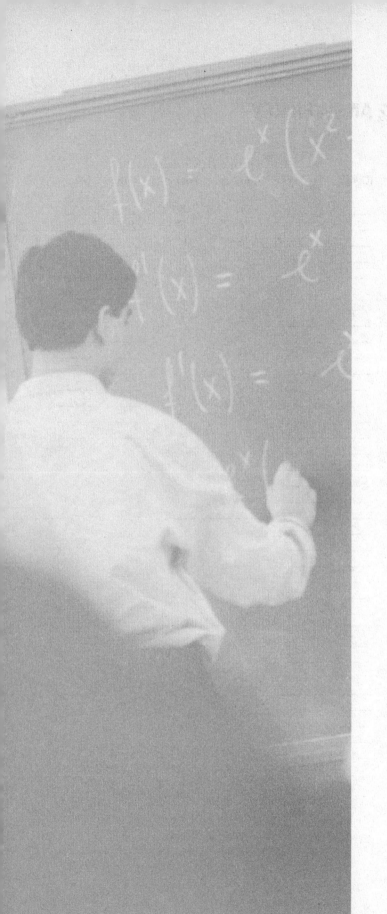

# Chapter 11
# Practice Test 2:
# Answers and
# Explanations

# PRACTICE TEST 2 ANSWER KEY

| Question number | Correct answer | Right | Wrong | Question number | Correct answer | Right | Wrong | Question number | Correct answer | Right | Wrong |
|---|---|---|---|---|---|---|---|---|---|---|---|
| 1. | B | ___ | ___ | 36. | A | ___ | ___ | 71. | B | ___ | ___ |
| 2. | D | ___ | ___ | 37. | B | ___ | ___ | 72. | D | ___ | ___ |
| 3. | C | ___ | ___ | 38. | B | ___ | ___ | 73. | C | ___ | ___ |
| 4. | A | ___ | ___ | 39. | B | ___ | ___ | 74. | B | ___ | ___ |
| 5. | A | ___ | ___ | 40. | C | ___ | ___ | 75. | C | ___ | ___ |
| 6. | D | ___ | ___ | 41. | C | ___ | ___ | 76. | C | ___ | ___ |
| 7. | C | ___ | ___ | 42. | B | ___ | ___ | 77. | B | ___ | ___ |
| 8. | B | ___ | ___ | 43. | D | ___ | ___ | 78. | A | ___ | ___ |
| 9. | C | ___ | ___ | 44. | A | ___ | ___ | 79. | B | ___ | ___ |
| 10. | A | ___ | ___ | 45. | B | ___ | ___ | 80. | D | ___ | ___ |
| 11. | A | ___ | ___ | 46. | D | ___ | ___ | 81. | B | ___ | ___ |
| 12. | A | ___ | ___ | 47. | B | ___ | ___ | 82. | D | ___ | ___ |
| 13. | C | ___ | ___ | 48. | C | ___ | ___ | 83. | D | ___ | ___ |
| 14. | A | ___ | ___ | 49. | C | ___ | ___ | 84. | D | ___ | ___ |
| 15. | C | ___ | ___ | 50. | D | ___ | ___ | 85. | A | ___ | ___ |
| 16. | D | ___ | ___ | 51. | B | ___ | ___ | | | | |
| 17. | B | ___ | ___ | 52. | C | ___ | ___ | | | | |
| 18. | C | ___ | ___ | 53. | C | ___ | ___ | | | | |
| 19. | A | ___ | ___ | 54. | A | ___ | ___ | | | | |
| 20. | D | ___ | ___ | 55. | D | ___ | ___ | | | | |
| 21. | C | ___ | ___ | 56. | D | ___ | ___ | | | | |
| 22. | B | ___ | ___ | 57. | C | ___ | ___ | | | | |
| 23. | C | ___ | ___ | 58. | D | ___ | ___ | | | | |
| 24. | D | ___ | ___ | 59. | C | ___ | ___ | | | | |
| 25. | C | ___ | ___ | 60. | A | ___ | ___ | | | | |
| 26. | B | ___ | ___ | 61. | C | ___ | ___ | | | | |
| 27. | A | ___ | ___ | 62. | C | ___ | ___ | | | | |
| 28. | A | ___ | ___ | 63. | C | ___ | ___ | | | | |
| 29. | D | ___ | ___ | 64. | A | ___ | ___ | | | | |
| 30. | A | ___ | ___ | 65. | B | ___ | ___ | | | | |
| 31. | D | ___ | ___ | 66. | A | ___ | ___ | | | | |
| 32. | B | ___ | ___ | 67. | B | ___ | ___ | | | | |
| 33. | C | ___ | ___ | 68. | D | ___ | ___ | | | | |
| 34. | C | ___ | ___ | 69. | D | ___ | ___ | | | | |
| 35. | D | ___ | ___ | 70. | A | ___ | ___ | | | | |

# PRACTICE TEST 2 EXPLANATIONS

The possible choices are examined for clues that should have indicated the correct answer. To help explain why a choice is right or wrong, resemblances between English and French words are noted, grammatical explanations are given, and an analysis of the comprehension questions is provided. Key words in the English translations of the questions are in **boldface**, as are the correct answers.

## Part A

| Question | | Answer | Key Word or Phrase | Fill In |
|---|---|---|---|---|
| 1 | The students are . . . the **teacher's explanation** of the test. | B | *avec l'enseignant* | in agreement with |
| 2 | Don't forget your **umbrella**; it's going to . . . tonight. | D | *parapluie* | rain |
| 3 | **There's nothing left** in the refrigerator. I have to . . . | C | *il n'y a plus rien* | go shopping |
| 4 | My . . . hurts from **typing on the computer** all day. | A | *d'avoir tapé sur l'ordinateur* | hand |
| 5 | His car keeps **breaking down** and he is really . . . | A | *est toujours en panne* | fed up |
| 6 | At dusk the sky . . . with a **thousand lights**. | D | *de mille feux* | sparkled |
| 7 | Commitments . . . need to be met, **or else people will not trust you.** | C | *sinon les gens ne vont pas faire confiance* | made |
| 8 | Jean is going to **buy books** at the . . . | B | *acheter* | bookstore |
| 9 | She is so **allergic** to dust that she . . . repeatedly. | C | *allergique* | sneezes |
| 10 | I opened a new . . . in the center of town **to sell cakes.** | A | *ou je vends des gâteaux* | business |
| 11 | He **fainted** when he heard . . . | A | *apprenant* | the news |
| 12 | **Nobody is answering the door**; she is probably not . . . | A | *personne ne répond* | there |
| 13 | I am very . . . that the **waiter is taking so long** with my order. | C | *garçon prend tellement de temps* | angry |

| Question | | Answer | Key Word or Phrase | Fill In |
|---|---|---|---|---|
| 14 | They have chosen to **live** . . . with their three young children. | A | *habiter* | in the suburbs |
| 15 | **They are full of energy** and are . . . every morning at 6. | C | *Ils sont pleins d'énergie* | up |
| 16 | I do not . . . . . to buy a new car since **I can ride my bicycle** into town. | D | *je peux me deplacer à vélo* | need (or desire) |
| 17 | For her **interview** with her future boss tomorrow, **she is going to wear** . . . | B | *elle va mettre* | suit |
| 18 | She has . . . **a lot of money** to buy her house. | C | *beaucoup d'argent* | borrowed |
| 19 | I suppose that you . . . since **the day was very hot.** | A | *la journée a été très chaude* | drink |
| 20 | He is **exhausted**; he has worked . . . | D | *exténué* | too much |
| 21 | The trains will **run less often** on. . . days. | C | *passent moins souvent* | holidays |
| 22 | This old map will . . . us **where the treasure is buried.** | B | *où le trésor est enterré* | show |
| 23 | **Years of use** will . . . **the leather** of these boots. | C | *années d'usage, cuir* | break in, wear out, soften |
| 24 | If I leave now, I can . . . **traffic jams.** | D | *les embouteillages* | avoid, miss |

**Part B**

| Question | Category | Answer | Explanation |
|---|---|---|---|
| 25 | Pronouns | C | (A) which—used for direct object pronouns, not subject<br>(B) to whom—*est* takes the subject and *mon père* is not an indirect object!<br>**(C) When not used as an interrogative pronoun, *lequel* can only be used with a preposition, (*avec lequel* or *pour lequel*)**<br>(D) of what/whom—*Le paquet* is not a possessive object |
| 26 | Prepositions | B | (A) at<br>**(B) correct—*pour*, here, means "in order to"**<br>(C) because<br>(D) after |
| 27 | Verbs | A | **(A) correct—the infinitive is required when a verb follows another verb**<br>(B) past participle—grammatically incorrect<br>(C) imperfect—grammatically incorrect<br>(D) present participle—grammatically incorrect |
| 28 | Prepositions | A | **(A) correct—*Belgique* is feminine**<br>(B) within—changes meaning<br>(C) *aux* is plural—grammatically incorrect<br>(D) *Belgique* is feminine; *du* can only be used with a masculine country (du Danemark, du Canada) |
| 29 | Adverbs | D | (A) the adverb *beaucoup* cannot be used before *bien*<br>(B) the adverb *beaucoup* cannot be used before *meilleur*<br>(C) makes no sense<br>**(D) correct—*mieux*, the comparative form of *bien*, may be preceded by *beaucoup*** |
| 30 | Past Participles | A | **(A) correct—the verb *mettre* takes *avoir*, so the past participle agrees with the direct object *robe*, placed before the verb**<br>(B) grammatically incorrect—no past participle agreement<br>(C) grammatically incorrect—no past participle agreement<br>(D) grammatically incorrect—infinitive |
| 31 | Conjunctions | D | (A) before: changes meaning<br>(B) since: followed by the indicative form of the verb<br>(C) although: changes meaning<br>**(D) correct—unless: followed by subjunctive form of the verb** |

| Question | Category | Answer | Explanation |
|---|---|---|---|
| 32 | Adverbs | B | (A) there<br>**(B) correct—where**<br>(C) toward<br>(D) near |
| 33 | Prepositions | C | (A) in<br>(B) during<br>**(C) correct—before**<br>(D) at |
| 34 | Conditional | C | (A) I will like—future; wrong tense<br>(B) I liked—imperfect: wrong tense<br>**(C) correct—conditional**<br>(D) no need for "que" and wrong tense |
| 35 | Pronouns | D | (A) makes no sense because *quelque* is not a pronoun<br>(B) little—makes no sense<br>(C) a little—*un peu* is used with something that is not numbered, i.e., *un peu de vin, de lait, de salade* . . . It would therefore be used after a question such as, *Est-ce que tu veux du vin, du lait, de la salade . . . ?*<br>**(D) correct— "one," *un* is used as a pronoun here** |
| 36 | Pronouns | A | **(A) correct—*y* replaces *à la poste*, which is a place**<br>(B) from there—*en* makes no sense with the verb *aller*; it can be used with *venir*: *j'en viens*<br>(C) always—makes no sense<br>(D) tomorrow—makes no sense |
| 37 | Verbs | B | (A) will swim: future—wrong tense!<br>**(B) correct—"had swum": indicates imperfect**<br>(C) has swum: *passé composé* —wrong tense<br>(D) would swim: present conditional—wrong tense |
| 38 | Subjunctive | B | (A) I went: imperfect—wrong tense<br>**(B) correct—subjunctive of the verb *aller* required after *il faut que***<br>(C) I will go: future—wrong tense<br>(D) I would go: conditional—wrong tense |

**Part C**

| Question | Category | Answer | Explanation |
|---|---|---|---|
| 39 | Vocabulary | B | (A) after—makes no sense<br>**(B) correct—since**<br>(C) for—makes no sense<br>(D) in—*dans* is not used before *le matin* |
| 40 | Adjectives | C | (A) all—would require the article *les*<br>(B) each one—makes no sense<br>**(C) correct—every**<br>(D) some—makes no sense |
| 41 | Pronouns | C | (A) grammatically wrong—*lui* is never a direct object<br>(B) grammatically wrong—*la* refers to *elle*, not *il*<br>**(C) correct—*le* is masculine and a direct object**<br>(D) grammatically wrong—*leur* is indirect and plural |
| 42 | Pronouns | B | (A) from there—*en* makes no sense here<br>**(B) correct—*y* refers to *les cafés***<br>(C) in—makes no sense<br>(D) where—makes no sense |
| 43 | Past Participles | D | (A) grammatically wrong—masculine ending<br>(B) grammatically wrong—infinitive<br>(C) grammatically wrong—plural feminine ending<br>**(D) correct—refers to *la foule*, which is feminine and singular** |
| 44 | Prepositions | A | **(A) correct—*s'adresser* takes *à* and means *parler à***<br>(B) toward—inappropriate<br>(C) with—makes no sense<br>(D) for—makes no sense |
| 45 | Verbs | B | (A) grammatically incorrect—past participle<br>**(B) correct—the infinitive is used after a preposition**<br>(C) grammatically incorrect—plural past participle<br>(D) grammatically incorrect—imperfect |

| Question | Category | Answer | Explanation |
|---|---|---|---|
| 46 | Prepositions | D | (A) through—makes no sense<br>(B) up to here—makes no sense<br>(C) at the—makes no sense<br>(D) correct—"to the end"; *bout* is a masculine noun and therefore needs the article *le*. *Jusqu'à* becomes *jusqu'au*—*jusqu'à* followed by a feminine noun would be *jusqu'à la* as in *jusqu'à la fin.* |
| 47 | Vocabulary | B | (A) head<br>(B) correct—back<br>(C) ear<br>(D) eyes |
| 48 | Vocabulary | C | (A) pulling<br>(B) carrying<br>(C) correct—shrugging<br>(D) passing |
| 49 | Prepositions | C | (A) ------- *continuer* requires a preposition<br>(B) for<br>(C) correct—*continuer à*<br>(D) in |
| 50 | Relative Pronouns | D | (A) ------- in French you may not omit a relative pronoun or a conjunction as you may omit "that" or "which" in English<br>(B) literally, the which<br>(C) whose—*dont* is wrong because *adresser* takes a direct object: *adresser une lettre*<br>(D) correct—direct object relative pronoun |
| 51 | Verbs | B | (A) subjunctive not needed here<br>(B) correct—*adresser* takes *avoir* and the correct tense is the *passé composé* in the first person<br>(C) will have—the future makes no sense here<br>(D) had—*avait*, wrong tense, wrong person |
| 52 | Present Participles | C | (A) wrong verb—need *être*, not *avoir*<br>(B) before—makes no sense<br>(C) correct—*rester* takes *être*; with a causative clause, you need the present participle<br>(D) was—makes no sense in the context |

| Question | Category | Answer | Explanation |
|---|---|---|---|
| 53 | Pronouns | C | (A) wrong—a formal letter requires *vous* <br> (B) me—this would refer back to the speaker <br> **(C) correct** <br> (D) him—there is no third party in the sentence |
| 54 | Prepositions | A | **(A) correct—the French expression is *prendre en consideration*** <br> (B) with <br> (C) by <br> (D) as |
| 55 | Pronouns | D | (A) wrong: *leur* is an indirect object pronoun, while *emmener* takes a direct object <br> (B) wrong: *emmener* starts with a vowel <br> (C) makes no sense because *emmener* is not a reflexive verb <br> **(D) correct—refers to the narrator; *emmener* starts with a  vowel and the *m'* is required** |
| 56 | Vocabulary | D | (A) maybe <br> (B) yet <br> (C) once—wrong because imperfect <br> **(D) correct—often** |

**Part D**

| Question | | Answer | Explanation |
|---|---|---|---|
| 57 | When the autumn rain arrived, the grandmother was | C | (A) "edgy"<br>(B) "sad"<br>(C) **correct: "glad"**—*accueillait du même soupir soulagé la pluie d'automne*—the grandmother "welcomed the autumn rain with the same sigh of relief"<br>(D) "proud" |
| 58 | During the summer months, Jacques | D | (A) "worked a lot"—familiar words, wrong context<br>(B) "spent his time reading"—no mention of reading in the text<br>(C) "never stopped having fun"—on the contrary, the text refers to Jacques's *ennui*<br>(D) **correct: "did not know how to entertain himself"**—key words *piétinements d'ennui* |
| 59 | When she was a little girl, the grandmother | C | (A) "had shorter vacations than Jacques"—she had no vacation at all: *Je n'ai jamais eu de vacances, moi.*<br>(B) "used to draw pictures during her free time"—no context for this<br>(C) **correct: "spent all her time working"**—*elle avait travaillé enfant, et travaillé sans relâche*<br>(D) "never did anything"—wrong: *elle avait travaillé sans relâche* |
| 60 | According to the passage, we understand that | A | (A) **correct: "Jacques continues his studies"**—*lorsque Jacques entra en troisième*<br>(B) "the grandmother does not want Jacques to keep going to school"—*Elle admettait que, pour un bénéfice plus grand, son petit-fils pendant quelques années ne rapporte pas d'argent à la maison.*—"She agreed that for a greater benefit, her grandson would not bring home any money for a few years."<br>(C) "the grandmother is opposed to Jacques's having a summer job"—no, since she says *Tu vas travailler cet été.*<br>(D) "Jacques is the third in his class"—familiar words—wrong context |

| Question | | Answer | Explanation |
|---|---|---|---|
| 61 | The grandmother wants Jacques to have a job so that he | C | (A) "might have some pocket money"—no context for this<br>(B) "might be able to pay for his studies"—no context for this<br>**(C) correct: "might contribute to the family expenses"**—*rapporter un peu d'argent à la maison*—**"bring home some money"**<br>(D) "might learn a trade:"—no context for this |
| 62 | The three-year-old child is crying because | C | (A) "he has lost his piece of chocolate"<br>(B) "he has hurt himself"<br>**(C) correct: "he does not know where his family is"**—*perdu*: lost<br>(D) "it is dark" |
| 63 | The shutters of the store are | C | (A) "open"<br>(B) "up"<br>**(C) correct:** *baissés*—**"pulled down"**<br>(D) "torn" |
| 64 | The woman "rushes to him" means that she goes toward the child | A | **(A) correct: "running"**<br>(B) "slowly"<br>(C) "crying"<br>(D) "unconcerned" |
| 65 | She "presses him tightly against her" means that she | B | (A) "pushes him away"<br>**(B) correct: "hugs him"**<br>(C) "smiles at him"<br>(D) "hits him" |
| 66 | Who does the woman think of as she carries the child away? | A | **(A) correct: "her own son"**—*en pensant à l'enfant qu'on n'a pas retrouvé*<br>(B) "the son of one of the refugees"<br>(C) "the reader's son"<br>(D) "the son of a guard" |
| 67 | The traffic jams mentioned in the text | B | (A) "are used to cork a bottle"—double meaning of the word *bouchon*, either a cork or a traffic jam<br>**(B) correct: "are traffic jams"**—**a street is** *embouteillée* **when it is jammed with cars**<br>(C) "delay the trains"<br>(D) "avoid wasting time" |

| Question | | Answer | Explanation |
|---|---|---|---|
| 68 | According to the text, the combination Train + Car Rental | D | (A) "is more expensive"<br>(B) "is too expensive"<br>(C) "is not very convenient"<br>(D) correct: "is a good deal"—*Tout en réalisant de vraies économies!* |
| 69 | According to this article, the French | D | (A) "go to the movies more and more often"<br>(B) "seldom go to the movies"<br>(C) "would rather watch television"<br>(D) correct: "enjoy watching movies at home more and more"—*Les Français auraient-ils attrapé le virus du home cinéma?* "Have the French caught the home-theater virus?" |
| 70 | The equipment linked to the home theater | A | (A) correct: "have more and more success"—*2002 devrait être l'année de l'explosion de ce marché en France*—"2002 should be the booming year of this market in France"<br>(B) "are not new"<br>(C) "are not very interesting"<br>(D) "are not in"—*être dans le vent* is a French idiom meaning *être à la mode* |
| 71 | Today, audiovisual equipment is | B | (A) "more expensive"<br>(B) correct: "cheaper"—*la baisse des prix*: lower prices<br>(C) "exorbitant"—literally "out of price"<br>(D) "prohibitive"—literally "that cannot be reached" |
| 72 | "The general public" represents | D | (A) "a few privileged people"<br>(B) "famous people"<br>(C) "film enthusiasts"<br>(D) correct: "most people" |

| Question | | Answer | Explanation |
|---|---|---|---|
| 73 | ". . . the manufacturers have more and more affordable products at their disposal" means that they | C | (A) "are getting rid of them"<br>(B) "need them"<br>(C) correct: "have access to them"—watch out! *Disposer de* here does not mean "to dispose of" but "to have at one's disposal." —i.e., *Je dispose de 1000 pour m'acheter un ordinateur* means "I have 1000 euros at my disposal to buy a computer."<br>(D) "make them" |
| 74 | When do you have to prepare the dough for the madeleines? | B | (A) "the next day"<br>(B) correct: "the day before"—*la veille*: the day before<br>(C) "two hours ahead of time"<br>(D) "yesterday" |
| 75 | According to the recipe, pastis is an ingredient which is | C | (A) "a must"<br>(B) "sweet"<br>(C) correct: "optional"—*facultatif*<br>(D) "fragrant" |
| 76 | "I have already hinted to you that" means "I have already" | C | (A) "told you"<br>(B) "repeated to you"<br>(C) correct: "suggested to you"<br>(D) "lied to you" |
| 77 | The hunchback has "big plans" because | B | (A) "he needs money right away"<br>(B) correct: "he thinks about his daughter's future"—*je dois assurer l'avenir de ma fillette*: "I have to secure my little girl's future"<br>(C) "he is a philosopher"<br>(D) "he loves money" |
| 78 | From the hunchback's speech, Ugolin remembers | A | (A) correct: "only the last words"—*De ce discours, Ugolin ne retint que les derniers mots. Ne . . . que* means "only."<br>(B) "maybe the first words"<br>(C) "always the last sentence"<br>(D) "everything but the end" |

| Question | | Answer | Explanation |
|---|---|---|---|
| 79 | In lines 18–23, after hearing the hunchback's plans, Ugolin is | B | (A) "amused"<br>(B) **correct: "very worried"**<br>(C) "full of joy"<br>(D) "reassured" |
| 80 | Ugolin is trying to find out whether the hunchback | D | (A) "is going to plant a vineyard"<br>(B) "will save the olive trees and the almond trees"<br>(C) "is planning to sell thistles"<br>(D) **correct: "knows about the existence of the spring"**—*il connaissait donc la source*: "so he knew about the spring" |
| 81 | "In every place" means | B | (A) "nowhere"<br>(B) **correct: "everywhere"**<br>(C) "somewhere else"<br>(D) "somewhere" |
| 82 | The convalescent runs the risk of breaking his other leg because the floor is | D | (A) "wet"<br>(B) "uneven"<br>(C) "full of holes"<br>(D) **correct: "slippery"**—*les salles sont cirées de telle façon qu'un convalescent, . . . doit se casser l'autre en tombant*—"the rooms are waxed in such a way that a convalescent . . . must fall and break the other one" |
| 83 | The courtyard in between every room is | D | (A) "full of sun"<br>(B) "without any shade"<br>(C) "sunny"<br>(D) **correct: "without any sun"**—*mais où le soleil ne vient jamais*: "but where the sun never comes" |
| 84 | In winter the patients' meals are | D | (A) "piping hot"<br>(B) "lukewarm"<br>(C) "at the right temperature"<br>(D) **correct: "very cold"**—*tout doit parvenir glacé*: icy cold |

| Question | | Answer | Explanation |
|---|---|---|---|
| 85 | Flaubert's tone in this passage is | A | (A) correct: "sarcastic"—Flaubert describes what he calls *la symétrie factice* ("the artificial symmetry") and *la propreté imbécile* ("the stupid cleanliness") of the arsenal<br>(B) "serious"<br>(C) "playful"<br>(D) "tragic" |

# HOW TO SCORE PRACTICE TEST 2

When you take the real exam, the proctors will collect your test booklet and bubble sheet and send your answer sheet to a processing center where a computer looks at the pattern of filled-in ovals on your answer sheet and gives you a score. We are providing you, however, with this more primitive way of scoring your exam.

## Determining Your Score

STEP 1    Using the answer key, determine how many questions you got right and how many you got wrong on the test. Remember: Questions that you do not answer do not count as either right answers or wrong answers.

STEP 2    Write the number of correct answers on line A.

(A) _____

STEP 3    Write the number of wrong answers on line B. Divide that number by 3.

(B) _____ ÷ 3 = _____

STEP 4    Subtract the number of wrong answers divided by 3 on line B from the number of correct answers on line A, and round to the nearest whole number. (C) is your **raw score**.

(A) _____ – (B) _____ = ( C ) _____

STEP 5    To determine your **real score**, look up your raw score in the left column of the Score Conversion Table on the next page; the corresponding score on the right is the score you earned on the exam.

# PRACTICE TEST 2
# SCORE CONVERSION TABLE

| Raw score | Scaled score | Raw score | Scaled score | Raw score | Scaled score |
|---|---|---|---|---|---|
| 85 | 800 | 45 | 630 | 5 | 410 |
| 84 | 800 | 44 | 620 | 4 | 410 |
| 83 | 800 | 43 | 620 | 3 | 400 |
| 82 | 800 | 42 | 610 | 2 | 400 |
| 81 | 800 | 41 | 610 | 1 | 390 |
| 80 | 800 | 40 | 600 | 0 | 390 |
| 79 | 800 | 39 | 600 | −1 | 380 |
| 78 | 800 | 38 | 590 | −2 | 380 |
| 77 | 800 | 37 | 580 | −3 | 370 |
| 76 | 790 | 36 | 580 | −4 | 360 |
| 75 | 790 | 35 | 570 | −5 | 360 |
| 74 | 780 | 34 | 570 | −6 | 350 |
| 73 | 780 | 33 | 560 | −7 | 350 |
| 72 | 770 | 32 | 560 | −8 | 340 |
| 71 | 770 | 31 | 550 | −9 | 340 |
| 70 | 760 | 30 | 550 | −10 | 330 |
| 69 | 760 | 29 | 540 | −11 | 330 |
| 68 | 750 | 28 | 540 | −12 | 320 |
| 67 | 740 | 27 | 530 | −13 | 320 |
| 66 | 740 | 26 | 530 | −14 | 310 |
| 65 | 730 | 25 | 520 | −15 | 300 |
| 64 | 730 | 24 | 520 | −16 | 290 |
| 63 | 720 | 23 | 510 | −17 | 290 |
| 62 | 720 | 22 | 500 | −18 | 280 |
| 61 | 710 | 21 | 500 | −19 | 280 |
| 60 | 710 | 20 | 490 | −20 | 270 |
| 59 | 700 | 19 | 490 | −21 | 270 |
| 58 | 700 | 18 | 480 | −22 | 260 |
| 57 | 690 | 17 | 480 | −23 | 260 |
| 56 | 690 | 16 | 470 | −24 | 250 |
| 55 | 680 | 15 | 470 | −25 through −28 | 240 |
| 54 | 680 | 14 | 460 | | |
| 53 | 670 | 13 | 460 | | |
| 52 | 660 | 12 | 450 | | |
| 51 | 660 | 11 | 450 | | |
| 50 | 650 | 10 | 440 | | |
| 49 | 650 | 9 | 430 | | |
| 48 | 640 | 8 | 430 | | |
| 47 | 640 | 7 | 420 | | |
| 46 | 630 | 6 | 420 | | |

# About the Authors

Monique Gaden, a graduate of the Université de Lyon, and Simone Ingram, a graduate of the Université de Lille, have taught French and English for many years.

# Practice Test 1 Form

Completely darken bubbles with a No. 2 pencil.  If you make a mistake, be sure to erase mark completely.  Erase all stray marks.

1. Ⓐ Ⓑ Ⓒ Ⓓ Ⓔ
2. Ⓐ Ⓑ Ⓒ Ⓓ Ⓔ
3. Ⓐ Ⓑ Ⓒ Ⓓ Ⓔ
4. Ⓐ Ⓑ Ⓒ Ⓓ Ⓔ
5. Ⓐ Ⓑ Ⓒ Ⓓ Ⓔ
6. Ⓐ Ⓑ Ⓒ Ⓓ Ⓔ
7. Ⓐ Ⓑ Ⓒ Ⓓ Ⓔ
8. Ⓐ Ⓑ Ⓒ Ⓓ Ⓔ
9. Ⓐ Ⓑ Ⓒ Ⓓ Ⓔ
10. Ⓐ Ⓑ Ⓒ Ⓓ Ⓔ
11. Ⓐ Ⓑ Ⓒ Ⓓ Ⓔ
12. Ⓐ Ⓑ Ⓒ Ⓓ Ⓔ
13. Ⓐ Ⓑ Ⓒ Ⓓ Ⓔ
14. Ⓐ Ⓑ Ⓒ Ⓓ Ⓔ
15. Ⓐ Ⓑ Ⓒ Ⓓ Ⓔ
16. Ⓐ Ⓑ Ⓒ Ⓓ Ⓔ
17. Ⓐ Ⓑ Ⓒ Ⓓ Ⓔ
18. Ⓐ Ⓑ Ⓒ Ⓓ Ⓔ
19. Ⓐ Ⓑ Ⓒ Ⓓ Ⓔ
20. Ⓐ Ⓑ Ⓒ Ⓓ Ⓔ
21. Ⓐ Ⓑ Ⓒ Ⓓ Ⓔ
22. Ⓐ Ⓑ Ⓒ Ⓓ Ⓔ
23. Ⓐ Ⓑ Ⓒ Ⓓ Ⓔ
24. Ⓐ Ⓑ Ⓒ Ⓓ Ⓔ
25. Ⓐ Ⓑ Ⓒ Ⓓ Ⓔ

26. Ⓐ Ⓑ Ⓒ Ⓓ Ⓔ
27. Ⓐ Ⓑ Ⓒ Ⓓ Ⓔ
28. Ⓐ Ⓑ Ⓒ Ⓓ Ⓔ
29. Ⓐ Ⓑ Ⓒ Ⓓ Ⓔ
30. Ⓐ Ⓑ Ⓒ Ⓓ Ⓔ
31. Ⓐ Ⓑ Ⓒ Ⓓ Ⓔ
32. Ⓐ Ⓑ Ⓒ Ⓓ Ⓔ
33. Ⓐ Ⓑ Ⓒ Ⓓ Ⓔ
34. Ⓐ Ⓑ Ⓒ Ⓓ Ⓔ
35. Ⓐ Ⓑ Ⓒ Ⓓ Ⓔ
36. Ⓐ Ⓑ Ⓒ Ⓓ Ⓔ
37. Ⓐ Ⓑ Ⓒ Ⓓ Ⓔ
38. Ⓐ Ⓑ Ⓒ Ⓓ Ⓔ
39. Ⓐ Ⓑ Ⓒ Ⓓ Ⓔ
40. Ⓐ Ⓑ Ⓒ Ⓓ Ⓔ
41. Ⓐ Ⓑ Ⓒ Ⓓ Ⓔ
42. Ⓐ Ⓑ Ⓒ Ⓓ Ⓔ
43. Ⓐ Ⓑ Ⓒ Ⓓ Ⓔ
44. Ⓐ Ⓑ Ⓒ Ⓓ Ⓔ
45. Ⓐ Ⓑ Ⓒ Ⓓ Ⓔ
46. Ⓐ Ⓑ Ⓒ Ⓓ Ⓔ
47. Ⓐ Ⓑ Ⓒ Ⓓ Ⓔ
48. Ⓐ Ⓑ Ⓒ Ⓓ Ⓔ
49. Ⓐ Ⓑ Ⓒ Ⓓ Ⓔ
50. Ⓐ Ⓑ Ⓒ Ⓓ Ⓔ

51. Ⓐ Ⓑ Ⓒ Ⓓ Ⓔ
52. Ⓐ Ⓑ Ⓒ Ⓓ Ⓔ
53. Ⓐ Ⓑ Ⓒ Ⓓ Ⓔ
54. Ⓐ Ⓑ Ⓒ Ⓓ Ⓔ
55. Ⓐ Ⓑ Ⓒ Ⓓ Ⓔ
56. Ⓐ Ⓑ Ⓒ Ⓓ Ⓔ
57. Ⓐ Ⓑ Ⓒ Ⓓ Ⓔ
58. Ⓐ Ⓑ Ⓒ Ⓓ Ⓔ
59. Ⓐ Ⓑ Ⓒ Ⓓ Ⓔ
60. Ⓐ Ⓑ Ⓒ Ⓓ Ⓔ
61. Ⓐ Ⓑ Ⓒ Ⓓ Ⓔ
62. Ⓐ Ⓑ Ⓒ Ⓓ Ⓔ
63. Ⓐ Ⓑ Ⓒ Ⓓ Ⓔ
64. Ⓐ Ⓑ Ⓒ Ⓓ Ⓔ
65. Ⓐ Ⓑ Ⓒ Ⓓ Ⓔ
66. Ⓐ Ⓑ Ⓒ Ⓓ Ⓔ
67. Ⓐ Ⓑ Ⓒ Ⓓ Ⓔ
68. Ⓐ Ⓑ Ⓒ Ⓓ Ⓔ
69. Ⓐ Ⓑ Ⓒ Ⓓ Ⓔ
70. Ⓐ Ⓑ Ⓒ Ⓓ Ⓔ
71. Ⓐ Ⓑ Ⓒ Ⓓ Ⓔ
72. Ⓐ Ⓑ Ⓒ Ⓓ Ⓔ
73. Ⓐ Ⓑ Ⓒ Ⓓ Ⓔ
74. Ⓐ Ⓑ Ⓒ Ⓓ Ⓔ
75. Ⓐ Ⓑ Ⓒ Ⓓ Ⓔ

76. Ⓐ Ⓑ Ⓒ Ⓓ Ⓔ
77. Ⓐ Ⓑ Ⓒ Ⓓ Ⓔ
78. Ⓐ Ⓑ Ⓒ Ⓓ Ⓔ
79. Ⓐ Ⓑ Ⓒ Ⓓ Ⓔ
80. Ⓐ Ⓑ Ⓒ Ⓓ Ⓔ
81. Ⓐ Ⓑ Ⓒ Ⓓ Ⓔ
82. Ⓐ Ⓑ Ⓒ Ⓓ Ⓔ
83. Ⓐ Ⓑ Ⓒ Ⓓ Ⓔ
84. Ⓐ Ⓑ Ⓒ Ⓓ Ⓔ
85. Ⓐ Ⓑ Ⓒ Ⓓ Ⓔ

# Practice Test 2 Form

Completely darken bubbles with a No. 2 pencil.  If you make a mistake, be sure to erase mark completely.  Erase all stray marks.

1.
YOUR NAME: _____
(Print)                                    Last                                                First                                    M.I.

SIGNATURE: _____                DATE: ____ / ____ / ____

HOME ADDRESS: _____
(Print)                                                        Number and Street

_____
                    City                                            State                                    Zip Code

(Print)

| | | | |
|---|---|---|---|
| 1. Ⓐ Ⓑ Ⓒ Ⓓ Ⓔ | 26. Ⓐ Ⓑ Ⓒ Ⓓ Ⓔ | 51. Ⓐ Ⓑ Ⓒ Ⓓ Ⓔ | 76. Ⓐ Ⓑ Ⓒ Ⓓ Ⓔ |
| 2. Ⓐ Ⓑ Ⓒ Ⓓ Ⓔ | 27. Ⓐ Ⓑ Ⓒ Ⓓ Ⓔ | 52. Ⓐ Ⓑ Ⓒ Ⓓ Ⓔ | 77. Ⓐ Ⓑ Ⓒ Ⓓ Ⓔ |
| 3. Ⓐ Ⓑ Ⓒ Ⓓ Ⓔ | 28. Ⓐ Ⓑ Ⓒ Ⓓ Ⓔ | 53. Ⓐ Ⓑ Ⓒ Ⓓ Ⓔ | 78. Ⓐ Ⓑ Ⓒ Ⓓ Ⓔ |
| 4. Ⓐ Ⓑ Ⓒ Ⓓ Ⓔ | 29. Ⓐ Ⓑ Ⓒ Ⓓ Ⓔ | 54. Ⓐ Ⓑ Ⓒ Ⓓ Ⓔ | 79. Ⓐ Ⓑ Ⓒ Ⓓ Ⓔ |
| 5. Ⓐ Ⓑ Ⓒ Ⓓ Ⓔ | 30. Ⓐ Ⓑ Ⓒ Ⓓ Ⓔ | 55. Ⓐ Ⓑ Ⓒ Ⓓ Ⓔ | 80. Ⓐ Ⓑ Ⓒ Ⓓ Ⓔ |
| 6. Ⓐ Ⓑ Ⓒ Ⓓ Ⓔ | 31. Ⓐ Ⓑ Ⓒ Ⓓ Ⓔ | 56. Ⓐ Ⓑ Ⓒ Ⓓ Ⓔ | 81. Ⓐ Ⓑ Ⓒ Ⓓ Ⓔ |
| 7. Ⓐ Ⓑ Ⓒ Ⓓ Ⓔ | 32. Ⓐ Ⓑ Ⓒ Ⓓ Ⓔ | 57. Ⓐ Ⓑ Ⓒ Ⓓ Ⓔ | 82. Ⓐ Ⓑ Ⓒ Ⓓ Ⓔ |
| 8. Ⓐ Ⓑ Ⓒ Ⓓ Ⓔ | 33. Ⓐ Ⓑ Ⓒ Ⓓ Ⓔ | 58. Ⓐ Ⓑ Ⓒ Ⓓ Ⓔ | 83. Ⓐ Ⓑ Ⓒ Ⓓ Ⓔ |
| 9. Ⓐ Ⓑ Ⓒ Ⓓ Ⓔ | 34. Ⓐ Ⓑ Ⓒ Ⓓ Ⓔ | 59. Ⓐ Ⓑ Ⓒ Ⓓ Ⓔ | 84. Ⓐ Ⓑ Ⓒ Ⓓ Ⓔ |
| 10. Ⓐ Ⓑ Ⓒ Ⓓ Ⓔ | 35. Ⓐ Ⓑ Ⓒ Ⓓ Ⓔ | 60. Ⓐ Ⓑ Ⓒ Ⓓ Ⓔ | 85. Ⓐ Ⓑ Ⓒ Ⓓ Ⓔ |
| 11. Ⓐ Ⓑ Ⓒ Ⓓ Ⓔ | 36. Ⓐ Ⓑ Ⓒ Ⓓ Ⓔ | 61. Ⓐ Ⓑ Ⓒ Ⓓ Ⓔ | |
| 12. Ⓐ Ⓑ Ⓒ Ⓓ Ⓔ | 37. Ⓐ Ⓑ Ⓒ Ⓓ Ⓔ | 62. Ⓐ Ⓑ Ⓒ Ⓓ Ⓔ | |
| 13. Ⓐ Ⓑ Ⓒ Ⓓ Ⓔ | 38. Ⓐ Ⓑ Ⓒ Ⓓ Ⓔ | 63. Ⓐ Ⓑ Ⓒ Ⓓ Ⓔ | |
| 14. Ⓐ Ⓑ Ⓒ Ⓓ Ⓔ | 39. Ⓐ Ⓑ Ⓒ Ⓓ Ⓔ | 64. Ⓐ Ⓑ Ⓒ Ⓓ Ⓔ | |
| 15. Ⓐ Ⓑ Ⓒ Ⓓ Ⓔ | 40. Ⓐ Ⓑ Ⓒ Ⓓ Ⓔ | 65. Ⓐ Ⓑ Ⓒ Ⓓ Ⓔ | |
| 16. Ⓐ Ⓑ Ⓒ Ⓓ Ⓔ | 41. Ⓐ Ⓑ Ⓒ Ⓓ Ⓔ | 66. Ⓐ Ⓑ Ⓒ Ⓓ Ⓔ | |
| 17. Ⓐ Ⓑ Ⓒ Ⓓ Ⓔ | 42. Ⓐ Ⓑ Ⓒ Ⓓ Ⓔ | 67. Ⓐ Ⓑ Ⓒ Ⓓ Ⓔ | |
| 18. Ⓐ Ⓑ Ⓒ Ⓓ Ⓔ | 43. Ⓐ Ⓑ Ⓒ Ⓓ Ⓔ | 68. Ⓐ Ⓑ Ⓒ Ⓓ Ⓔ | |
| 19. Ⓐ Ⓑ Ⓒ Ⓓ Ⓔ | 44. Ⓐ Ⓑ Ⓒ Ⓓ Ⓔ | 69. Ⓐ Ⓑ Ⓒ Ⓓ Ⓔ | |
| 20. Ⓐ Ⓑ Ⓒ Ⓓ Ⓔ | 45. Ⓐ Ⓑ Ⓒ Ⓓ Ⓔ | 70. Ⓐ Ⓑ Ⓒ Ⓓ Ⓔ | |
| 21. Ⓐ Ⓑ Ⓒ Ⓓ Ⓔ | 46. Ⓐ Ⓑ Ⓒ Ⓓ Ⓔ | 71. Ⓐ Ⓑ Ⓒ Ⓓ Ⓔ | |
| 22. Ⓐ Ⓑ Ⓒ Ⓓ Ⓔ | 47. Ⓐ Ⓑ Ⓒ Ⓓ Ⓔ | 72. Ⓐ Ⓑ Ⓒ Ⓓ Ⓔ | |
| 23. Ⓐ Ⓑ Ⓒ Ⓓ Ⓔ | 48. Ⓐ Ⓑ Ⓒ Ⓓ Ⓔ | 73. Ⓐ Ⓑ Ⓒ Ⓓ Ⓔ | |
| 24. Ⓐ Ⓑ Ⓒ Ⓓ Ⓔ | 49. Ⓐ Ⓑ Ⓒ Ⓓ Ⓔ | 74. Ⓐ Ⓑ Ⓒ Ⓓ Ⓔ | |
| 25. Ⓐ Ⓑ Ⓒ Ⓓ Ⓔ | 50. Ⓐ Ⓑ Ⓒ Ⓓ Ⓔ | 75. Ⓐ Ⓑ Ⓒ Ⓓ Ⓔ | |

**NOTES**

NOTES

# NOTES

# NOTES

NOTES

NOTES

NOTES

NOTES

NOTES

NOTES

NOTES